HOW TO USE FEELING VERY
GOOD AS A WAY INTO THE
HAPPINESS ZONE

HOW TO USE FEELING VERY GOOD AS A WAY INTO THE HAPPINESS ZONE

Gilbert George Pennant Junior

© 2017 Gilbert George Pennant Junior
All rights reserved.

ISBN: 1999871707
ISBN 13: 9781999871703

Contents

Preface The Tale of Two Queens, Sources of Inspiration · · · · · · · · ·ix
Acknowledgments · xiii
Introduction The Benefits of Happiness· xv
    Act "as if." In other words, fake it until you make it. · · · · · · · · · · · xvii

1 What Makes You Happy? · 1
    Reflection Pause · 1
    The Path to Contentment· 2
    Happiness Bank · 3
    Happy Goals · 5
    Your needs will be identified from the outer circle
    (page 2 The path to Contentment diagram)· · · · · · · · · · · · · · · · 6
    Your desires will be identified from the outer circle
    (page 2 The path to Contentment diagram)· · · · · · · · · · · · · · · · 7
    Mind· 7
    Body · 7
    Spirit/Soul · 8
    Past Participant Profile · 8
    What Makes You Happy? · 9
2 Lifetime Happiness Plan · 10
    Reflection Pause · 10
    Past Participant Profile · 13
    Life-Life Balance · 13

3	Setting SMART Happy Goals	17
	3.1 What Are Goals?	17
	What Are SMART Goals?	17
	Reflection Pause	18
	Barriers That Prevent You from Achieving Your Goals	20
	Factors That Help You Achieve Your Goals	21
	This information will be helpful to complete Appendix 5: Happy SMART Goal-Setting Sheet, SMART Happiness Goal Help, page 7 of 7	21
	Common Mistakes in Setting Goals	24
	Working on SMART Goals	24
	How Often Do You Have to Do a Particular Task?	24
	Past Participant Profile	25
	How Long Must You Spend on a Particular Task?	25
4	Creating the Happiness Goals Monitor	27
	Specific, Measurable Steps	27
	Reflection Pause	27
	How to Measure Progress	28
	Reflection Pause	28
	Past Participant Profile	30
5	Monitoring and Evaluation of Happiness Goals	31
	Daily Monitor	32
	Reflection Pause	33
	Reached Daily Happiness Target	34
	Below Your Daily Happiness Target	34
	Weekly Monitor	34
	Past Participant Profile	35
	Week 1	36
	Week 2	37
	Week 3	38
	Week 4	39
	Week 5	40
	Monthly Monitor	41

	Month 1	41
	Monthly Monitor	42
	Yearly Monitor	43
6	Adjustment to the Happiness Goals Monitor	44
	Daily/Weekly Adjustment to the Happiness Goal Monitor	44
	Over performing	44
	Meeting Your Target	44
	Past Participant Profile	45
	Not Meeting Your Target	45
	Week 5	46
	Monthly Adjustment to the Happiness Goal Monitor	47
	Yearly Adjustment to the Happiness Goal Monitor	47
	Reflection Pause	48
7	Conclusion	49
	Reflection Pause	49
8	Appendix	50
	Appendix 1: Contentment	50
	Appendix 2: Maslow's Hierarchy of Needs	51
	Maslow's Hierarchy of Needs	52
	Examples in Use	53
	Characteristics of Self-Actualized People	53
	Appendix 3: Lifetime Happiness Plan 1	56
	Appendix 4: Contentment Goals list	58
	Appendix 5: Happy SMART Goal-Setting Sheet 1 of 7	59
	Appendix 6: Edward De Bono's Six Thinking Hats	66
	Thinking Hat 1	66
	Thinking Hats 2	67
	Thinking Hats 3	68
	Appendix 7: Testimonials from Past Participants	69
	Appendix 8: Author Biography	71
	Appendix 9: Daily/Weekly Happiness Goals Monitor	72
	Appendix 10: Monthly Happiness Goals Monitor	73
	Appendix 11: Yearly Happiness Goals Monitor	74

Appendix 12: Weekly happiness goals adjustment monitor · · · · 75
Appendix 13: Monthly happiness goals adjustment monitor · · · 76
Appendix 14: Yearly Happiness Goals Adjustment Monitor · · · 77
Appendix 15: Glossary · 78
Feeling Very Good savings account · 78
Gilism · 78
Happiness Bank · 78
Happiness Zone · 78
Lifetime Happiness Plan · 78
Life-Life balance · 78
SMART Happy Goals · 79
Appendix 16: Bibliography · 80
Appendix 17 Learning objectives for anyone reading this book · · 82
Appendix 18: Pleasant and Unpleasant Feelings · · · · · · · · · · · · 83
Appendix 19: Other training and coaching programs on offer: · · · 87
Notes page · 93

Preface

The Tale of Two Queens, Sources of Inspiration

The tale of two queens is about my mother, who has always been royal to me, and the mother of Her Royal Highness Queen Elizabeth II of the United Kingdom, formerly known as the Queen Mother.

Gilbert George Pennant Jr. and his mother, Eunice Pennant, at a birthday celebration

Some of my inspiration has come from these two mothers, my own and the Queen's mother, whom I had the privilege of meeting when I was manager of Mitcham Citizens Advice Bureau (general advice center) in 1989 when she visited the bureau.

How to use Feeling Very Good as a way into the Happiness Zone

*The late Queen Mother talking with Gilbert George Pennant Jr.
when she visited Mitcham Citizens Advice Bureau in 1989*

My mother is one of the few people I know who has achieved everything that she wanted to in her life. She successfully brought up her seven children. She lives in the Happiness Zone.

I wonder if the Queen Mother appreciated how much happiness her royal visits gave to the people of Mitcham. I experienced this phenomenon firsthand when she visited the bureau that I was managing in 1989. I never got the opportunity to ask her this question. It would be great to ask her children, grandchildren, or great-grandchildren.

The Queen Mother was popular with the public, earning the nickname "Smiling Duchess" because of her consistently indomitable spirit. She was of great moral support to the British public during both world wars. After World War II, the Queen Mother became the royal family's matriarch. She continued to travel and make public appearances in the United Kingdom and throughout the Commonwealth, and she didn't allow personal illness to slow her down until the end of her life.

The methodology used in this book relies in part on the skills I learned in acquiring a diploma in management qualification, which is managed by the Chartered Management Institute United Kingdom. The course, made up of eight units, covers all of the fundamental principles of operational management. Included are units on the following topics: managing financial and nonfinancial resources, effective financial management, managing marketing activities, effective communication and information management, managing performance, developing personnel and personnel performance, developing and managing yourself, and planning to meet customer and quality requirements. My neurolinguistic programming (NLP) qualification has also influenced the process described in this book. NLP is an approach to communication, personal development, and psychotherapy created by Richard Bandler and John Grinder in California in the 1970s. NLP's creators claim there is a connection between neurological processes (*neuro*), language (*linguistic*), and behavioural patterns learned through experience (*programming*), and that these can be changed to achieve specific goals in life.

I have used my overall experience to provide you with straightforward principles for figuring out what makes you happy and how to stay in the Happiness Zone, which is a state of contentment.

I have also applied my knowledge as a qualified chair-based exercise instructor to write and deliver training sessions on happiness.

Acknowledgments

The most important and inspirational people to me in the writing of this book have been my parents, my family, and my friends.

A special thanks to my daughters, Diana, Felicia, and April-Louise, for their help as my critiquing partners in the development of this book.

I thank my wife, Angela, for her continued support.

I am grateful to everyone with whom I've had the pleasure of working, either as a participant or in other ways. Without their contributions, this work would not have been completed.

In my view, contact with people is one of the key components of happiness and it has helped me to conceive, create, devise, and write this book.

Introduction

The Benefits of Happiness

I am not always happy. I choose to not always be sad. I developed an approach to encompass a better way of being, which is contentment. This was important in the writing of this book, as I wanted a balanced approach to my life.

Also, I consider the journey to be as important as the final destination. For reasons outside your control, you might have to take a different route than originally anticipated, or the time frame you planned may have to be extended. So while on your journey, it may be wise to enjoy the now.

One day, I asked myself if I was happy. I thought I was, but I wanted to be sure. I decided to write down what I thought made me happy (goals). Then I wrote down the steps that I could undertake to meet those goals. I developed a daily, weekly, monthly, and annual monitor to confirm that I was taking the steps to achieve my goals; this document became the Happiness Goals Monitor.

I worked on the principle that if I did all of the tasks on my list, I would subconsciously experience continuous happiness while doing them. I reflected back at the end of any given period (usually daily) to confirm that I was in an ongoing state of happiness. Knowing that I was working toward my goals helped me to understand that I was happy in the past (the whole day) as well as in the moment (the present). It provided me with encouragement that I could continue to be happy in the future.

If I wasn't able to do an activity on my list, I tried to understand why and do something about it. I discovered that taking action to work on maintaining my happiness made me feel happy.

The focus of this book is to help you work out what makes you happy and monitor it on a daily basis to make sure that you are focusing on it.

You may find that what you thought would make you happy doesn't once you have achieved it. Having that knowledge is a good thing, because you can change the goal and move toward something else until you identify the actual things that make you happy. You then monitor to ensure that you are focusing on those things.

Your objective is to make sure that you complete your daily, weekly, monthly, and yearly activities, which you add up. That number becomes your target score. The closer you are to you target score, the happier you will be.

While I was writing this book, I smiled a lot because I was focusing on what made me happy. The more I thought about the Happiness Monitor (the process to check that you doing things that make you feel good), the more opportunities I had to continuously feel happy.

As I was writing this book and researching various aspects, it became apparent to me that there is already a wealth of information out there on happiness. I will give you the key points. If anything stirs your curiosity, then seek out more information. Anything that helps you to work on your goals will contribute to your happiness. Action as opposed to inaction helps you to stay in the Happiness Zone, a state of contentment.

If someone is told that he has a limited amount of time left to live, he focuses on what he has always wanted to do and makes it happen—he goes on an amazing holiday or parachutes out of an airplane. You get the idea! The truth is that you do have a limited amount of time to live. It reminds me of the tale of a person who jumped off a skyscraper, and as he was falling to the ground, someone asked him how he was doing, and he replied, "So far, so good." Until he hit ground, he was doing well. It could be argued that we are all free-falling to the earth. Therefore, you can choose to make the most of your time now!

You can only live one moment at a time, in the present. The past will give you memories, which you remember and may influence your action now. The future is what you imagine may happen in a particular situation;

anticipating how it will turn out may cause you stress. If you have unhappy memories, deal with them. Seek professional help, if you need to.

Choose to use good memories as a foundation to move forward. If you are worrying about the future, do something different now so that an unpleasant event does not happen. Focus on the present—on the now!

Concentrate on tasks that are under your control. What can you do now to move toward being happy?

Choose to have a balance. It's unwise to have eating chocolate every day as a goal if another goal is to be healthy. Eat chocolate in moderation to a level that does not negatively impact your health.

ACT "AS IF." IN OTHER WORDS, FAKE IT UNTIL YOU MAKE IT.
William James is regarded by many as the father of American psychology. He is credited with introducing the concept of "acting as if" in a lecture titled "The Will to Believe," published in 1897. In it, he states that when you "act as if" you already have the quality or object you desire, your subconscious mind, which is your servomechanism (your servant), receives the command and immediately acts upon it without judgment. Your subconscious mind is like software—what you program into it will be the output. While this technique is very simple, it is also highly effective and backed by research from the field of neuroscience.

You and I have something in common. We both want continuous happiness. The question is: Is that possible?

I have added the word "continuous" intentionally. I believe that it is possible to achieve happiness and maintain it, and this book will give you the tool to stay in the Happiness Zone, which is contentment.

The *English Oxford Living Dictionaries* defines *happiness* (noun) as "the state of being happy."

The *English Oxford Living Dictionaries* defines *happy* (adjective) as "feeling or showing pleasure or contentment."

Cultures around the world and throughout history have considered the issue of happiness. Written evidence of the psychological and philosophical search for happiness dates back twenty-five hundred years to the writings of Confucius, Buddha, Socrates, Aristotle, and many others. Lawrence Ogbo Ugwuanyi,[1] states that Africans have different philosophies than Westerners do. From this view, he considers how a person can lead a life full of joy and happiness surrounded by a family that support one's decisions in life, without material blessings[1].

The American Declaration of Independence of July 4, 1776, states that the pursuit of happiness is a constitutional right.

'We hold these truths to be self-evident, that all men are created equal, that they are endowed by their Creator with certain unalienable Rights that among these are Life, Liberty and the pursuit of Happiness.'

His Holiness Tenzin Gyatso, the fourteenth Dalai Lama of Tibet, who is the spiritual and political leader of the Tibetan people, says this about happiness:

'Happiness is determined more by the state of one's mind than by one's external conditions, circumstances or events—at least once one's basic survival needs are met.'

Happiness can be achieved through the systematic training of our hearts and minds, through reshaping our attitudes and outlook.

My definition of happiness can best be described by a story I heard long ago, I forget where. An older bee flew up to younger bee and asked, "Why are you chasing your wing in a circle?"

The younger bee said, "I have concluded that my wing is happiness, and I want to catch it."

The older bee said, "I have found that wherever I go, my wing comes with me." In other words, if you do something that makes you feel good, happiness will be right there too!

I consider that overall happiness is made up of many different elements. I have endeavored to understand how to obtain it over my lifetime. Like many of you, I've read many self-help books, listened to recordings, and watched films.

---

1 Lawrence Ogbo Ugwuanyi, "The Question of Happiness in African Philosophy," *South African Journal of Philosophy* 33 (December 2014): 513–522, http://dx.doi.org/10.1080/02580136.2014.976755.

How to use Feeling Very Good as a way into the Happiness Zone

On April 2, 2012, the first United Nations conference on happiness and well-being took place at the UN headquarters in New York. The April meeting was convened by the Himalayan Kingdom of Bhutan, which, in the 1970s, introduced the concept of gross national happiness (GNH). It began measuring GNH in 2008, looking at factors such as living standards, health, education, culture, good governance, and psychological well-being.

In this context, Bhutan describes happiness not as relating to an everyday passing mood, but as "the deep, abiding happiness" that comes from living in harmony with the natural world and with others—that is, from "feeling totally connected with our world."

Jigmi Y. Thinley, then prime minister of Bhutan, explained, "Gross national happiness is the philosophy or development paradigm that has guided Bhutan's development in a way that has been holistic and based on the belief that the aspiration, the ultimate goal of every human individual, is happiness. So then it must be the responsibility of the state, or the government, to create those conditions that will enable citizens to pursue this value, this goal."

To mark the conference, a new[2] World Happiness Report was released. The report reflected a new worldwide demand for more attention to happiness and to absence of misery as criteria for government policy. It reviewed the state of happiness in the world at that time and showed how the new science of happiness explains personal and national variations in happiness. The following were among the key findings:

- The happiest countries in the world are all in Northern Europe (Denmark, Norway, Finland, and Netherlands, etc.). Their average life evaluation score is 7.6 on a scale of 0–10.
- The least happy countries are all poor countries in Sub-Saharan Africa (Togo, Benin, Central African Republic, Sierra Leone) with average life evaluation scores of 3.4.

---

2 The 2012 World Happiness Report, published by The Earth Institute, http://worldhappiness.report/download/

- It is not just wealth that makes people happy. Political freedom, strong social networks, and an absence of corruption are together more important than income in explaining well-being differences between the top and bottom countries.
- At the individual level, good mental and physical health, someone to count on, job security, and stable families are crucial.
- Over time as living standards have risen, happiness has increased in some countries, but not in others (for example, the United States). On average, the world has become a little happier in the last thirty years.
- Unemployment causes as much unhappiness as bereavement or separation do. At work, job security and good relationships do more for job satisfaction than high pay and convenient hours.
- Mental health is the biggest single factor affecting happiness in any country. Yet only a quarter of mentally ill people get treatment for their conditions in advanced countries and fewer in poorer countries.
- Stable family life and enduring marriages are important for the happiness of parents and children.
- In advanced countries, women are happier than men, while the position in poorer countries is mixed. Happiness is lowest in middle age.

How to use Feeling Very Good as a way into the Happiness Zone

On June 28, 2012, the United Nations General Assembly adopted by consensus March 20 as the International Day of Happiness. On this date each year, a universal phenomenon occurs. The sun is on the same plane as the earth's equator, so day and night are of equal length, creating balance in the earth's celestial coordinate systems. It is an annual global day of awareness and activities that will drive increasing levels of connectivity, education, and action-based programs. [3]Countries around the world are considering how to measure happiness and feeding the result into policy.

At the time of this writing, this information will be out of date. The world Database of Happiness has 6,984 publications in its bibliography of happiness, of which 3,460 report empirical investigations using accepted measures of happiness. There are 755 measures of happiness used in 1,457 studies. There are 14,463 correlation findings observed in 1,454 studies, excerpted from 1,104 publications. There are about twice as many findings still to be entered.

Happiness is a complicated concept and means different things to different people. What works for one person may not work for another person. This book is the culmination of my detailed exploration of the topic. It provides you with a tool to assess whether you are in a state of continuous happiness, and if you are not, describes how you can get to and stay in the Happiness Zone, a state of contentment.

The process described in this book is easy to use and understand. It is based on the feedback of participants in the training sessions that I have delivered over the years. Based on evidence, I believe that once you have developed a Lifetime Happiness Plan (a document that sets out what makes you feel good and what your needs and desires are over a lifetime) you will be empowered for life.

---

3 "International Day of Happiness 20 March," accessed November 17, 2017, http://www.un.org/en/events/happinessday/.

Let us start from the position that you can be happy now. The happiness monitor is a mechanism to confirm that you are happy by showing that you have done the tasks associated with all of your goals each day.

You can only live in the present, so it's not worth dwelling in the past or in the future.

If you are overweight because you ate too much in the past, you can become healthier in the future if you change your behavior now, in the present. Therefore, by concentrating on the present by working toward your goals, you will be closer to achieving the overall aim of being healthier: happiness. However, you do not need to be healthy to be happy. You can be terminally ill and still be happy.

When cultivated, happiness brings us closer to what is "good" in humanity and benefits everyone, including friends, family, neighbours, colleagues, and communities at large.

Governments, workplaces, community groups, and schools are more interested in happiness and well-being than ever before, and for good reason. Positive psychology, the scientific study of optimal functioning, has gained momentum over the past decade, as its scientifically grounded interventions have proved to have long-lasting effects on health, work, and personal relationships.

We now know that positive emotions play a vital role in our well-being in all aspects of our lives. Positivity increases curiosity and creativity, increases motivation and engagement, and undoes the negative effects of negative emotions. For example, blood pressure and pulse rate will drop more quickly after one is stressed.

Happy people live longer, have better immune systems, and suffer less depression, anxiety, and cardiovascular disease. Happy people are more resilient and successful in life. And it doesn't end there.

Being happy at work seems to have a great return on investment. Disengagement and stress in the workplace leak out into personal relationships and have detrimental effects on our health and well-being. The costs to society and communities are huge.

The research is clear. Cultivating a positive mind-set at work enables greater innovation. Employees are better team players, earn more, and have better relationships with colleagues and managers. Positive workplaces have lower absenteeism, lower turnover rates, and—what employers want to hear—higher productivity.

Cultivating empathy and gratitude goes a long way in building relationships socially and at work, which we know is vital to our happiness levels.

Focusing on our own strengths and on the strengths of others, building optimism, increasing awareness, reducing negative emotions, cultivating positive ones, setting meaningful goals, and living in the moment are crucial to our well-being.

The first stage to creating your own happiness monitor is to work out what makes you feel good and how many individual activities you have to undertake each day see figure below *Example of a level of happiness score*. This number becomes your target score. You will compare it with the number of activities you do in a day, which will be your actual score. The closer these two scores are to one another, the happier you will be and the closer you will be to getting into and staying in the Happiness Zone, the state of contentment.

In the illustration of a happiness score, see figure below *Example of a level of happiness score*. If this person undertakes five activities each day (the activities will be explained later as the example is expanded throughout the book) and then multiplies that figure by seven days a week, four/five weeks a month, and twelve months a year, he or she will arrive at target scores for any given period of time.

Name:		Date:
Level of Happiness	Goals target activities	Goals target engagement duration
Happiness daily target	5.1	Different length of time for each goal see daily/weekly monitor
Happiness weekly target	36	28 hours
Happiness monthly target	156	121 hours
Happiness annual target	1,872	1,456 hours

Example of a level of happiness score

If a person undertakes the number of activities in the goal target column for the duration of time listed in the goal target duration column and maintains these scores, she will be continuously happy—in the happiness zone, which is contentment.

After completing the first draft of this book, I was concerned that it should not be theoretical, untested work. Therefore, I took the program out into the community to test it. From 2012 to present, my clients have included the United Kingdom (UK) government and local government and national and local charities in the UK. I have delivered the program on which this book is based to the following groups:

- youths
- ex-offenders (youths and adults)
- youths with autism
- people suffering from mild mental illness
- unemployed people
- employed people
- self employed
- Business owners

- men
- women
- caregivers (people who look after disabled or sick family members or clients)
- people of various sexual orientation
- others

I can say with confidence that the process has changed the lives of the majority of people with whom I have worked.

Chapters 1–6 take you through an example of creating, monitoring, and adjusting a Lifetime Happiness Plan. Chapter 8 contains blank copies of the forms that you can use to create your own Lifetime Happiness Plan, and the forms to monitor and adjust to make sure that you have reached the Happiness Zone and are staying there!

1

What Makes You Happy?

The illustration below: *The path to contentment* is an overview of the whole process, the path to contentment. What makes you feel good will be identified from the outer circle of your Happiness Bank. What your needs are will be identified from your Happy Goals outer circle. Maslow's Hierarchy of Needs has proven to be a useful tool to give people a framework for looking at their needs. I considered using "Nain's Hierarchy of Needs: An Alternative to Maslow's & ERG's Hierarchy of Needs," but that was more appropriate for organizational use rather than an individual perspective.

What your desires are will be identified from your Happy Goals outer circle.

Once you have identified the information from the outer circles, the combination of those activities will lead you to continuous happiness, which is the inner circle of contentment.

REFLECTION PAUSE

I worked one-to-one with a woman on my 'Manage Yourself to be Valuable in the Workplace program', and at the beginning of most sessions, she asked me how I was feeling that day. I mostly answered. "Fantastic." She found this answer perplexing, as she considered that it was impossible to always be happy. She was right; I'm not always happy. However, I realized that I was grateful to be alive, and no matter what situation I was in, it could be worse. Therefore, I choose to have a positive rather than a negative outlook on my existence. I am the optimistic pessimist!

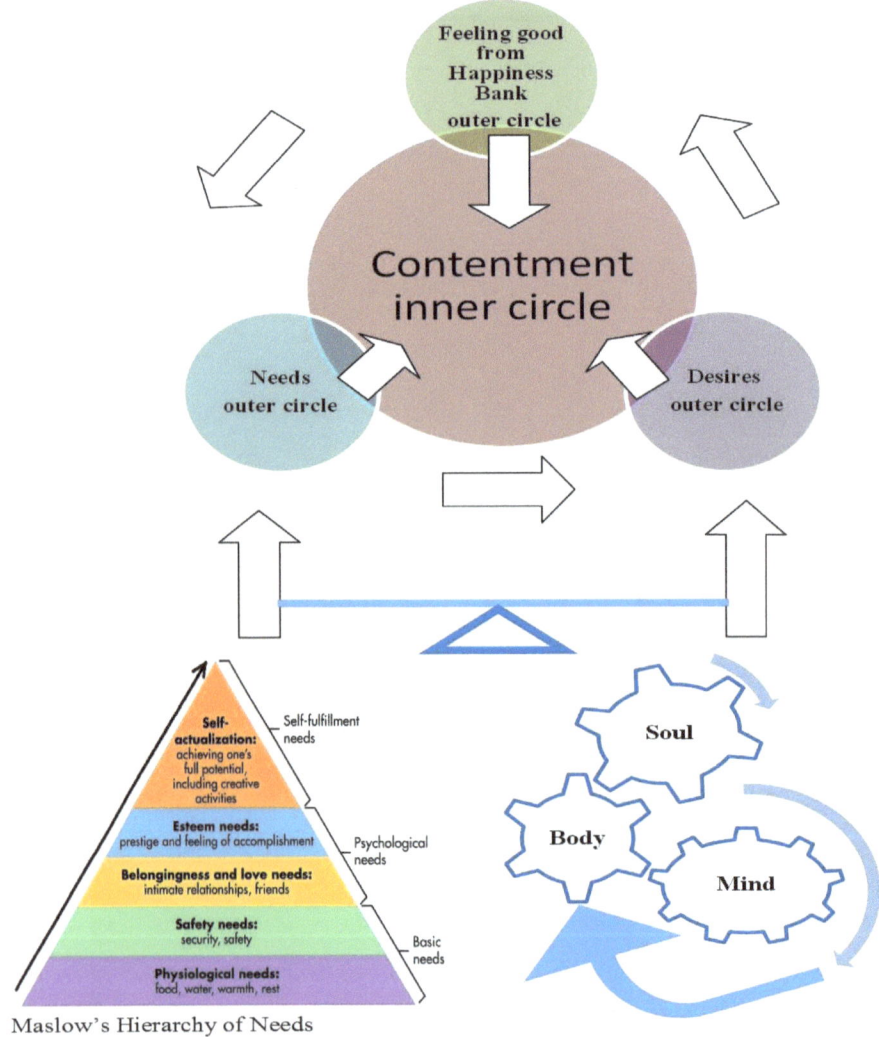

The Path to Contentment

What makes you happy can be anything that makes you feel good when you think about it. When you engage with that thing, emotions create a positive effect on you that puts you in the Happiness Zone, giving you the energy and motivation to do anything you want to. That is how you use happiness as a tool for change.

By focusing on things that make you feel good, you work on your Happy Goals (needs and desires) to create the life you want, which leads to contentment.

List what makes you happy under the headings below. Feel free to add as many different headings as you want to. What makes you feel good will be identified from your Happiness Bank's outer cycle. Your needs will be identified from your Happy Goals outer circle. Your desires will be identified from your Happy Goals outer circle

What makes you feel good will be identified from your Happiness Bank's outer circle. When thinking about what makes you feel good, consider what emotions come up. The feelings and emotions are what you want to concentrate on; that is the energy that will motivate and empower you to achieve anything you want in life.

HAPPINESS BANK

The Happiness Bank is where you open your Feeling Very Good savings account. You deposit anything that makes you feel good in it—good memories, past success, music, gratitude, etc.

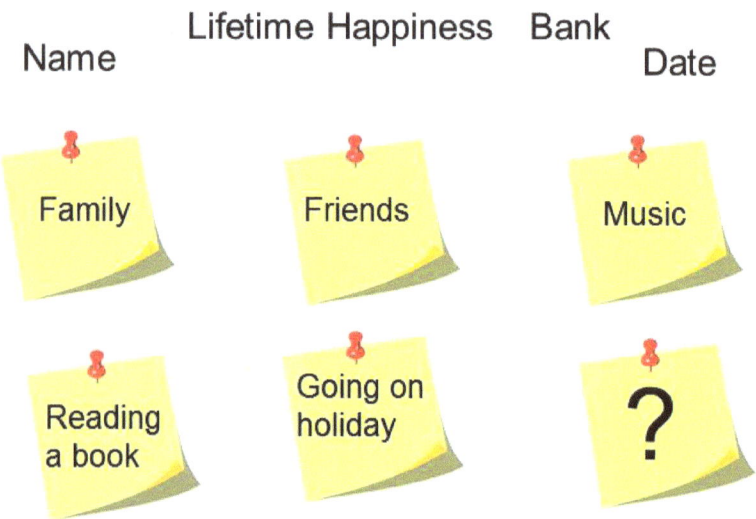

Example of a lifetime Happiness Bank

An added bonus to your saving account is that whenever you do not feel 100 per cent, you can make a withdrawal of something that makes you feel good to change your state to a happy one. You take something out of the account by choosing something from the list and engaging in it. You can make a deposit at any time, adding factors that come into your consciousness or any new activity that you have experienced.

How to use Feeling Very Good as a way into the Happiness Zone

Example of a Feeling Very Good savings bank account

HAPPY GOALS

What your needs are will be identified from your outer circle. What your desires are will be identified from your outer circle. Now list everything you feel would give you the life you want if you had it or experienced it.

Example of setting goals for things you need or desire

This list of Happy Goals can be divided into two groups:

- needs
- desires

YOUR NEEDS WILL BE IDENTIFIED FROM THE OUTER CIRCLE (PAGE 2 THE PATH TO CONTENTMENT DIAGRAM)

In training sessions, some people have difficulty identifying the factors that would make up their perfect lives. I've found Maslow's hierarchy of needs to be a useful framework to help participants think of their needs and categorize them. Once a person has addressed his or her needs, he or she can move on to desires. What I consider particularly perceptive about Maslow's hierarchy of needs (see Appendix 2: Maslow's Hierarchy of Needs) is that, although he has placed needs in order of priority, he states that a person does not have to stick to his priority schedule. If you want to achieve your needs in a different order, you can choose to do so. Or if you want to partially complete a need before moving to another one, you are free to do so. Maslow is just suggesting a structure as a starting point.

YOUR DESIRES WILL BE IDENTIFIED FROM THE OUTER CIRCLE (PAGE 2 THE PATH TO CONTENTMENT DIAGRAM)

This is where you can use your imagination and think about your desires—the sky is the limit. Think big—the bigger, the better. During training sessions, I have used the following headings as a starting point:

- mind
- body
- soul/spirit

I believe that these headings describe our totality as human beings, and each one is connected to yet independent of the others. Functioning effectively requires each part to operate at its maximum efficiency. Therefore, these headings may give you an outline to ensure that your desires list covers most things. However, if you feel that something you desire does not fit under any of these headings, create a new one and use it.

MIND

Anything you think you desire belongs on this list. Most participants mainly focus on material things and people, ranging from a better car to the ideal relationship. Good mental health, from a mind point of view, is also important to ensure that you are prepared for the challenges of now.

BODY

Choose to look after your body. Have regular medical checkups, consider your diet, and undertake sufficient exercise. Good physical health will be important (in most cases) to achieve all of your goals, not just your desires. Treat your body with respect, and it will serve you well.

You may want to strive to be a specific weight and to eat better food. Write these items down. Let your imagination flow. Improving the condition of your body increases your chances of achieving your goals. However, even if your body is not in perfect condition, you can still reach contentment.

SPIRIT/SOUL

Reflecting on your existence and taking time out are important parts of the picture. You can create this list from a religious point of view, if you like. Include anything that relaxes you and gives you peace—for example, listening to music or taking a nature walk.

PAST PARTICIPANT PROFILE

A is in his late forties, and his problems started nearly thirty years ago when his second daughter died of bronchitis pneumonia. He and his then partner blamed themselves for the loss of their child, and his drinking and drug taking, which started with cannabis and then shifted to heroin and crack, increased. He worked for twenty-three years as a street cleaner for a London council, where he was also a union shop steward. Unfortunately, he was diagnosed with osteoarthritis, and his employment was terminated. In 2008, he left his partner and was living on benefits and renting rooms in the Newham area of London. In 2010, he decided that he no longer wanted to be dependent on drugs and alcohol and sought help to deal with his substance abuse. In 2011, he was evicted from his room. He managed to get a bed in a homeless-persons' shelter, where he has been living for two years while seeking permanent housing. A has not taken drugs since 2011.

After attending one of my programs for homeless people, his results were as follows:

- *He was setting clear goals and targets to move forward.*
- *He was attending weekly gym sessions.*
- *He was eating healthier meals.*

WHAT MAKES YOU HAPPY?

You now have a list of what makes you Feel Very Good, and your Needs list is divided into three sections, as suggested by Maslow's hierarchy of needs: basic needs, psychological needs, and self-fulfilment needs. Your Desires list is divided under three headings: mind, body and soul/spirit.

In the next chapter, we look at how to empower yourself for life by creating your Lifetime Happiness Plan.

2

Lifetime Happiness Plan

The Lifetime Happiness Plan helps you think about and then visualize and actualize all of the pieces that make up your picture of happiness/contentment in one place. It's divided into three sets of goals: Feeling Very Good goals, Needs goals, and What You Desire goals.

The Lifetime Happiness Plan begins with your overall objective—contentment—and works backward to where you are now. It helps you to set out the direction, priorities, goals, and time frame to go forward with your plan.

It provides you with answers to the following questions:

- Where are you now (the pre-assessment)?
- Where do you want to get to?
- What information should you monitor along the way as you move toward your destination (the post-evaluation)?

It helps you to identify changes in your environment that result from changes in the way that you do things. You will analyse them to determine if the change is what you want. If not, you'll do something different.

REFLECTION PAUSE

When I was working as a civil servant, I thought being in a more senior role would contribute to my happiness. (I was not just thinking about the money; I wanted to be part of management, the decision-making process.) To achieve that aim, I set the goal to gain a relevant qualification. I was happy while working toward the qualification. When I got it, a diploma in management, it did help my career, but it did not get me to where I wanted to be. When I achieved the goal, I was able to remove it from my list, which made me feel very good.

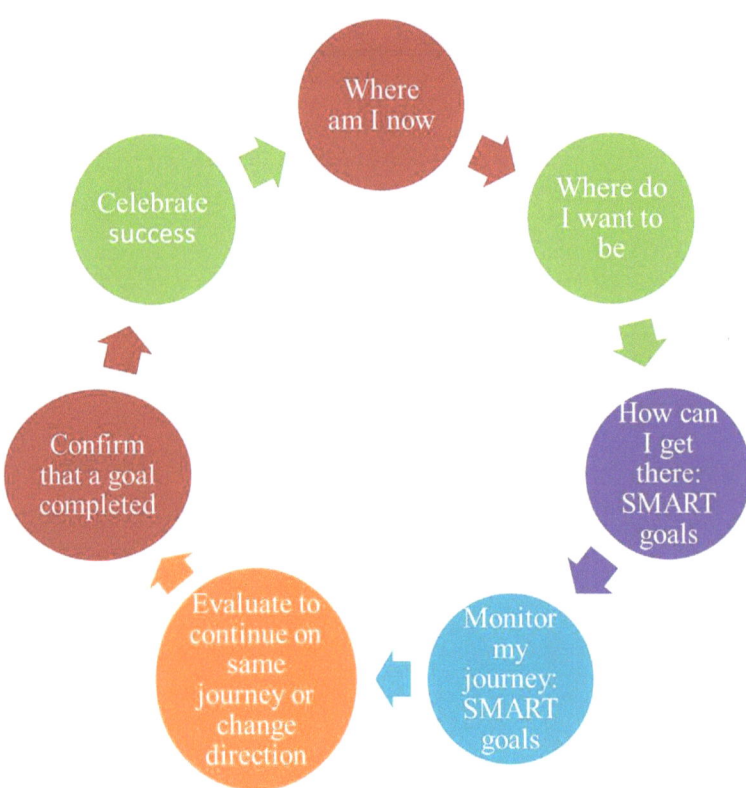

Where am I now in the process cycle?

1. What makes you happy?
2. What do you need to exist?
3. What are your desires?
4. Are you being honest with yourself?
5. Are you willing to take responsibility for your actions?
6. Time frame: six months to two years. At the end of that time frame, start another time frame.

The plan has been designed to use over a lifetime, so it may change from period to period. As you achieve some goals, new ones will emerge. It is a document that you can refer to often and will give you your overall recipe for happiness. It also has the flexibility to be amended based on your experiences, what you learn, and your environment. It helps confirm that each goal does fit together to create the picture of contentment that you want. Each person's plan will be different even if some elements are the same.

The Lifetime Happiness Plan encourages you to use your five senses (sight, hearing, taste, smell, and touch) when you write down the goals and time frame. The other part of the plan is where individuals are encouraged to draw, paint, or make a collage of images that correspond to the words. The other senses are to be included in whatever way you want, as the more of your senses you use, the more vivid the picture becomes.

PAST PARTICIPANT PROFILE

C is in her late thirties and she is married and a mother to 2 children. She is a successful office manager. However, she has always wanted to run her own business.

After attending one of my programs her outcomes were as follows:

She created her own Lifetime Happiness plan.

She undertook other training courses to provide her with skills and knowledge in her chosen field.

She started to work part time in her job, while developing her business.

She now is successfully running her own business

She is now working on the other goals in her Lifetime Happiness plan

LIFE-LIFE BALANCE

The *Cambridge Dictionary* defines work-life balance as "the amount of time you spend doing your job compared with the amount of time you spend with your family and doing things you enjoy." I believe a different way to express this concept is choosing to have a **Life-Life balance.**

Diagram of a balanced life.

Work is important, but it does not represent 50 percent of your existence. It can be included as a needs goal—that is, you need to undertake some kind of work to gain money or goods to exchange for food, shelter, etc.

Fill in your Lifetime Happiness Plan. Place your Feeling Very Good goals, your Needs goals, and your What You Desire goals under the relevant headings. You now determine which ones you do first, second, etc. A good way to do that is to consider how soon you want to achieve something.

The first goal to work on is one in your Feeling Very Good goals list. These goals will motivate and inspire you to complete the rest.

How to use Feeling Very Good as a way into the Happiness Zone

Lifetime Happiness Plan:- Contentment, page 1 of 2 Express using your five main senses: Sight, Hearing, Taste, Smell, and Touch.		

Name: Signature: Date:

Time line	Feel Very Good goals	Needs goals Basic, Psychological, and Self-fulfilment	Desire goals Mind, Body and Soul/Sprit
Within 6 months	Family	Financial/job Health	
Within in a year	Pray & meditate Friends	Nurture social relationships Gratitude Say thank you like you mean it	Exercise Career
Beyond	Smile even when you don't feel like it	Family	Spirituality, pray & meditate

Example of a completed Lifetime Happiness Plan (page 1 of 2)

Lifetime Happiness Plan:- Contentment, page 2 of 2
Express using your five main senses: Sight, Hearing, Taste, Smell, and Touch.

Name: Signature: Date:

Example of a completed Lifetime Happiness Plan (page 2 of 2)

In reality, you will have different time frames in which to complete your goals. But for the purpose of this book, all of the goals in the example below are to be achieved in one year.

3

Setting SMART Happy Goals

3.1 WHAT ARE GOALS?

A goal sets out the steps to taken to achieve an aim. The more detail you can include in each of the steps on your journey, the better the chance of success. The purpose of a range of goals is to contribute to an overall objective, which, in the Happiness Zone, is to reach a feeling of contentment. (See the glossary for a detailed explanation.)

To complete your goals, you choose to undertake several actions, which must all be SMART (specific, measurable, achievable, realistic/relevant, and timed).

I consider the SMART goal approach to be as good as any other tool for tracking, monitoring, evaluating, and adjusting your behaviour when necessary. I've found that this approach is easy to explain during training sessions, as most participants already have knowledge of it.

WHAT ARE SMART GOALS?

Specific: A specific goal has a much greater chance of being accomplished than a general goal does. To set a specific goal, you must answer the six "W" questions:

- Who is involved?
- What do I want to accomplish, and what are the steps?
- Where: Identify a location.
- When: Establish a time frame.

- Which: Identify requirements and constraints.
- Why: List the specific reasons, purpose, or benefits of accomplishing the goal.

Example: A general goal would be regular exercise, but a specific goal would be join a gym and work out three days a week.

What specific steps are you going to take? In some training sessions, I've found that participants have already taken various steps to achieve a goal without success. They are therefore unclear or simply do not know what to do differently to reach their goals, and they struggle to list new or different steps.

Introducing parallel thinking, as developed by Edward de Bono (see Appendix 6), into training sessions has proved to be a helpful tool in some cases. Individually or in a group, de Bono's Six Thinking Hats provide a framework to consider a new or revised approach to achieving a goal.

In group sessions, participants working on each other's goals learn the Six Thinking Hats technique, which they can use on their own goals. This allows the collective experience and intelligence of the group to be tapped.

REFLECTION PAUSE

During one training course, one person set a goal to lose weight, which included the activity of regular attendance at a gym. However, he did not have the money to pay the subsidized gym entrance fee for unemployed people. Another participant in the course advised him that in some cases, one can get a doctor's referral to use the gym, which would cover the gym fee and proceeded to explain the process.

Measurable: When you monitor your progress, you know where you are in your journey. I have found that every step that you successfully achieve will generate a feeling of euphoria, spurring you on to the next step until you reach you goal.

To determine if your goal is measurable, consider the following questions:

- How much or how many?
- How will I know when it is accomplished?

Record the answers, as you want to measure your actions against them.

Attainable: When you identify the goals that are most important to you, you begin to work out ways you can reach them. You develop the attitudes, abilities, skills, and financial capacity to reach them. You begin seeing previously overlooked opportunities to bring yourself closer to the achievement of your goals.

You can attain almost any goal when you plan your steps wisely and establish a time frame that allows you to carry out those steps. Goals that may have seemed far away and out of reach eventually move closer and become attainable—not because your goals shrink, but because you grow and expand to match them. When you list the steps to achieve your goals, you build your self-image. You see yourself as worthy of those goals and develop the traits and personality that allow you to reach them.

Realistic/Relevant: To be realistic, a goal must represent an objective that you are both willing and able to work towards. A goal can be both challenging and realistic. You are the only one who can decide just how high your goal should be. But be sure that every goal represents substantial progress.

A challenging goal is frequently easier to reach than an easy one is, because an easy goal exerts low motivational force. Some of the hardest jobs you have ever accomplished actually seem easy simply because they are labours of love.

A goal must be relevant to your life and other priorities. If it's a "should" inherited from someone else or out-of-date thinking, ditch or revise it.

Timely: There is no sense of urgency without a time frame. If you want to lose twenty pounds, when do you want to lose it by? "Someday" won't work. But if you attach it to a time frame, such as "by August 30," then you've set your unconscious mind into motion to begin working on the goal.

Your goal is probably realistic if you truly *believe* that it can be accomplished. Additional ways to know if your goal is realistic is to determine if you or someone else has accomplished anything similar in the past. Or ask yourself what conditions would have to exist to accomplish this goal.

T can also stand for tangible. A goal is tangible when you can experience it with one of the senses—that is, taste, touch, smell, sight, or hearing. When your goal is tangible, you have a better chance of making it specific, measurable, and thus, attainable.

Example: If your aim is continuously being happy, one goal to work on in pursuit of that aim is to be healthier. Activities that will promote that goal include eating healthy food and exercising regularly.

Here are some reasons why setting goals is important:

- A goal gives you direction.
- By writing the goal down, you now have a clear path of where you want to go.
- It energizes you.
- It inspires you to take the action.

BARRIERS THAT PREVENT YOU FROM ACHIEVING YOUR GOALS

This information will be helpful to complete Appendix 5: Happy SMART Goal-Setting Sheet, SMART Happiness Goal Barriers, page 6 of 7.

1. Information or skill gap. You don't know what you don't know! If you're going for a big goal, you may find it worthwhile to invest in expert help. Experts might be consultants who can teach you how to run your small business more effectively, teachers who can give you weekly music lessons, life coaches who can give you new insights into your behaviour, and so on.
2. You're not using the following principles:
   - cause and effect
   - perception is projection
   - results vs. reasons (if you are not getting the results you want, do something different)

3. Negative emotions are getting in the way. They include:
   - anger
   - sadness
   - fear
   - hurt
   - guilt
4. Values are misaligned. Values are abstract, ranked in order of importance, and dynamic concepts that essentially describe what we desire or seek to achieve. We may hold values like loyalty, truthfulness, charity, service, and many others.
5. You hold limiting beliefs. Limiting beliefs are those which constrain us in some way. Just by believing them, we do not think, do or say the things that they inhibit; and in doing so we impoverish our lives.
6. You have no goal or a wrongly formed goal—that is, it is not SMART.
7. You have taken no decisive, determined, persistent action.

FACTORS THAT HELP YOU ACHIEVE YOUR GOALS

THIS INFORMATION WILL BE HELPFUL TO COMPLETE APPENDIX 5: HAPPY SMART GOAL-SETTING SHEET, SMART HAPPINESS GOAL HELP, PAGE 7 OF 7

1. You

    You are your greatest asset therefore use yourself to make it happen! This might mean praising yourself when you're doing well or encouraging yourself to keep going when things are tough. You might need a sympathetic ear or a pat on the back.
2. A "happy ratio" of ten to one. According to the Nobel Prize-winning scientist Daniel Kahneman, each day we experience approximately twenty thousand moments. A moment is defined as a few seconds in which our brain records an experience. The quality

of our days is determined by how our brains recognize and categorize our moments—either as positive, negative, or just neutral. Rarely do we remember neutral moments. There is no question that the memories of our lives are recorded in terms of positive and negative experiences.

Now scientists propose that each day, our brains—i.e., our thoughts and emotions—keep track of our positive and negative moments, and the resulting score contributes to our overall mood. Over the past decade, scientists have explored the impact of positive-to-negative interaction ratios in our work and personal lives. They have found that this ratio can be used to predict—with remarkable accuracy—everything from workplace performance to divorce.

Therefore, to offset a negative moment, you need a ten-to-one ratio of positive moments. For every one negative comment, you need ten positive ones (in my opinion).

3. Family and friends. If you tell your family and friends that you're going to lose thirty pounds in the next year, you've made a public commitment. As time goes by, they might ask you how you're progressing. When you're tempted to eat a candy bar or dig into a bag of chips, that accountability can be enough to give you the willpower boost that you need.
4. Other people. While family and friends can be a real support, they won't always be able to give you advice that can help you toward your goal. Look around for people who can—like-minded individuals working toward a similar goal to yours.
5. Values. Values are abstract, ranked in order of importance, and dynamic concepts that essentially describe what we desire or seek to achieve. We may hold values such as loyalty, truthfulness, charity, service, and many others.
6. Beliefs. Beliefs are judgments about ourselves and the world around us. They are usually generalizations. A typical belief may be "killing is bad." Notice that the belief includes not only an action or thing ("killing") but a judgment about that action or thing ("is bad").

7. No plan B. Choose to express goals with no alternatives; in war, when lives are at stake, there is no alternative to victory. Seldom is there the same life-or-death consequence in the everyday world, but the stakes can feel just as high sometimes. When setting a goal, choose to express it with a firm, all-or-nothing way of thinking. A soft goal isn't really a goal at all; it's a hope. You can *hope* to be successful, or you can *plan* to be successful. Setting goals with no alternatives leads to the success you deserve.

COMMON MISTAKES IN SETTING GOALS

People often make the following mistakes when they set goals:

- The goals are too big.
- The goals are not specific.
- There are too many goals.
- The goals are not written down.

WORKING ON SMART GOALS

You have identified and prioritized your goals for your Lifetime Happiness Plan under three main headings: Feeling Very Good goals, Needs goals, and Desire goals.

Start by focusing on the goals listed in the first time frame of your Lifetime Happiness Plan. You may find that many of the tasks associated with your goals are already part of your daily life. Therefore, you may be doing some of these activities, or you may not need to make significant changes to meet a goal.

Example: Saying "thank you" like you mean it. If being grateful is one of your goals, there are many opportunities in daily life to achieve it—when speaking to family, friends, or colleagues; when getting served in a shop; the list is endless.

For other goals, you may need to set time aside to work on the activities involved.

Example Exercise: Set aside times each week to work out to achieve this goal.

HOW OFTEN DO YOU HAVE TO DO A PARTICULAR TASK?

In the "what" section of your SMART goal sheet (appendix 5), you have listed the steps to be taken to move toward completing a particular goal. You then have to work out how often you will engage in a task to complete it—daily, weekly, monthly, or yearly—and the amount of time you are going to spend on each step. After the first monitoring period, it will be clear whether you are devoting enough time to a particular task.

In the example on page 26 'Example of a 'contentment goals' duration list', under the column: **Goals target daily engagement duration,** I've estimated how long a person might engage in working toward a goal in each work session.

In the example on page 29 of 'Example of a 'contentment goals' frequency list', under the column: **Goals target weekly activities frequency,** I've estimated the number of times a person will spend on the activities associated with each goal. If you want to work on a goal daily, then it will be seven times each week. If you want to work on a goal less frequently, then work out how many times a week you will do it. You then multiply up or down, according the frequency you want. You will be able to change how often you do something based on the information you get from your Happiness Monitor.

PAST PARTICIPANT PROFILE

C is forty-eight years old, and he was the full-time caregiver for both of his parents. Unfortunately, his mother passed away in 2005, and his father passed away in 2011. He is still grieving the losses. C has a bad back, a bad knee, and a bad hip, and he takes medication for depression. C is married with four children, and apart from his immediate family, he has not established a social network, as he was a full-time caregiver for twenty-five years. After the program, he had the following outcomes:

- *He was able to maintain regular attendance.*
- *He engaged with other members of the group.*

HOW LONG MUST YOU SPEND ON A PARTICULAR TASK?

The goal and the activities associated with it will determine the amount of time necessary.

Example: You are seeking a new career or job. One week, this may involve searching for suitable vacancies. Another week, it may require spending two hours to complete an application form.

Below is an example of what a "contentment goals" list could look like. Note that in the examples being used throughout the book, all of the goals have target-achievement dates within one year.

Contentment goals list	Goals target achievement date	Goals target weekly activities		Goals target daily engagement duration
Career	2 year	X1	Weekly	1 hour
Financial	3 year	X1	Weekly	1 hour
Family	6 months	X2	Weekly	2 hours
Nurturing social relationships	1 year	X7	Weekly	7 hours
Health	6 months	X7	Weekly	7 hours
Exercise	1 year	X3	Weekly	3 hours
Gratitude Say Thank You Like You Mean It	6 months	X7	Weekly	2 hours
Smile Even When You Don't Feel Like It	6 months	X7	Weekly	2 hours
Spirituality, Pray & Meditate	1 year	X1	Weekly	1 hours
Play and have fun	2 years	X1	Weekly	2 hours

Example of a "contentment goals" duration list

In Chapter 3: Setting SMART Happy Goals, I have included a list of the barriers that prevent you from achieving your goals and a list of the factors that help you to achieve your goals. The list is not exhaustive. Use this information to complete the last two pages of your Happy SMART Goal worksheets, which is located in Appendix 5.

4

Creating the Happiness Goals Monitor

Select the goals you will work on first from your Lifetime Happiness Plan (see chapter 2). Transform the goals that you have chosen into Happy SMART goals **(See Chapter 3: Setting SMART Happy Goals)**.

SPECIFIC, MEASURABLE STEPS

For each Happy SMART goal, list the actual steps that you will take to progress toward achieving your goals. It does not matter if you do not have all the steps needed to reach your journey's end or do not know what the next step is.

REFLECTION PAUSE

Edward De Bono's Six Thinking Hats may be a helpful tool to assist you in this area. See Appendix 6.

When you start to think about each step, consider what action you have to take to complete it. You then have to estimate how much time over a week (seven days) you will spend on the task. It does not matter if you do not complete the task within a week. You just need to know what you intend to achieve each week and record the progress on the SMART goal-specific "step sheet" in Appendix 5, 2 of 7.

You may find that when you complete one step, the results of that step suggest that you have to go in a direction different from your original plan. Therefore, flexibility is recommended in your approach. The same SMART goal-specific "step sheet" in Appendix 5, 2 of 7 is to be used to record action that is to be taken, the duration of time to be spent on the step, and the results, which may inform the action of the next step.

HOW TO MEASURE PROGRESS

In the box of the SMART goal-specific "step sheet" in Appendix 5, 2 of 7, you record how you will know when each step has been completed. You now have the information that you will use to set up your Happiness Monitors, appendices 9, 10 & 11.

It is recommended that you complete the Happiness Monitor on regular a basis—daily or weekly—whether you completed tasks or not. The advantage of updating the Happiness Monitor on a daily basis is even if you don't complete all the actions for a particular day, you can fill in the comments box with your observations while they are fresh in your mind.

Monitoring on a regular basis helps to identify the areas in which you are not hitting your targets on a daily basis. It is important to understand why you are not completing the tasks you set for yourself and then do something about it.

After each time period, review your progress to determine what has been achieved and what is still outstanding. Also, identify any goals you have on the list that you no longer want to achieve. Pruning the list is a good thing. It does not matter that you are changing your goals as long as you are moving toward something. As life progresses, it is perfectly possible that you will evolve and no longer want what you wanted in the past.

REFLECTION PAUSE

I used to work in banking. When I decided to apply for another job, I started to wear smarter clothes to work because I attended interviews during my lunch hour, planning to be gone from that employer soon. I started to feel better about myself. My colleagues started to notice that I was looking smarter and being friendlier. They began to treat me differently. In fact, I was offered a more senior job, but I decided to leave anyway. In my subconscious, I was acting as if I was in a better job, which in turn led me to get a better one.

Contentment goals list	Goals target achievement date	Goals target weekly activities frequency		Goals target daily engagement duration
Career	1 year	X1	Weekly	1 hour
Financial	1 year	X1	Weekly	1 hour
Family	1 year	X2	Weekly	2 hours
Nurture social relationships	1 year	X6	Weekly	7 hours
He alth	1 year	X7	Weekly	7 hours
Exercise	1 year	X4	Weekly	3 hours
Gratitude Say Thank You Like You Mean It	1 year	X6	Weekly	2 hours
Smile Even When You Don't Feel Like It	1 year	X6	Weekly	2 hours
spirituality, Pray & Meditate	1 year	X1	Weekly	1 hours
Play and have fun	1 year	X1	Weekly	2 hours
Weekly target		36		28 hours
Monthly target		180		140 hours
Yearly target		2,160		1,680 hours

Example of a "contentment goals" frequency list

Use the information in the above example to complete the daily/weekly Happiness Monitor.

Daily/Weekly

Happiness monitor		Daily/weekly monitor							Totals	
Goal	Frequency	Mon	Tue	Wed	Thu	Fri	Sat	Sun		
Health	Daily X 7	Yes	Yes	Yes	Yes	Yes	Yes	Yes	7	
Totals		1	1	1	1	1	1	1	Actual 7	Target 7

Example of a completed daily/weekly Happiness Monitor

PAST PARTICIPANT PROFILE

P was his forties and came to the United Kingdom from Poland in 2005 as a qualified chef. He initially stayed with friends in a rented room and then moved into another one with a partner. He was able to get regular temporary work as a chef from an employment agency. After two years his relationship ended, and his partner left the rented rooms, leaving him with significant debts. When he could no longer get work from the employment agencies, his landlord asked him to leave. He became homeless, sleeping in different churches, before he managed to get a bed in Anchor House (a homeless shelter), where he has been living for the last year while seeking permanent housing. After attending the program, he had the following outcomes:

- *He was setting clear goals and targets to move forward.*
- *He was attending weekly Happy sessions.*
- *He was looking for full-time employment.*

5

Monitoring and Evaluation of Happiness Goals

Without measuring results, you cannot confirm that you have been continuously happy in the Happiness Zone, contentment, for the last period. Monitoring allows you to identify and record areas that need improvement and determine why you did or didn't achieve a target score. You learn whether you're in the Happiness Zone or not.

Evaluation works in partnership with monitoring. The monitoring method signals whether target scores are being met, and then a good evaluation can help clarify where you are in the process. In the evaluation, you will draw conclusions about why the scores are the way they are. If you met your target, how should you continue? If you didn't, what action you are going to take to move forward?

You want to concentrate on the changes in your environment and how they affect your feelings, which will require continuous commitment, time, and effort. Once you have set up your Happiness Monitor, the challenge is to maintain it.

Evaluation informs you if you are in the Happiness Zone over a given period of time. It helps you to understand what you did right and what you need to work on. It allows you to review the way that you are working on your goals. You also will be able to identify unintended results. Therefore, effective evaluation provides lessons and highlights significant accomplishments and other ways of moving forward.

The steps of monitoring and evaluation include the following:

- Select your goals.
- Make your goals SMART.
- Select activities to achieve the goals, which will be the output indicators to monitor.
- Gather baseline information on your current position in relation to the goals.
- Regularly collect data to assess whether the targets are being met.
- Analyze and record results.

Adjust your monitor after the evaluation to take into account your findings. If you did not achieve all the tasks that were set for a day, you may be able to make them up during the week. However, do not carry tasks forward to the next week.

If you are not completing all tasks in a given time on a regular basis, this will be picked up in the weekly/ monthly/annual monitors. You will have to understand why you are not reaching your target scores. You can change the way you work, **accept that you are not going to achieve that goal, amend the goal, or remove it.**

You can change your emotional state to a happy one by thinking about the steps you have set to reach your goals (over a day, week, month, or year) and where you are in the process. Just thinking about the fact that you are working toward making yourself happy gives you a focus and a direction. It can motivate and inspire you to keep going.

DAILY MONITOR

At the end of each day, ask yourself if you have completed all of your tasks for that day. If you're not sure how to answer for a specific task of a certain goal; if you are leaning toward yes, then the answer is yes. If it is more no than yes, then answer no, for example consider starting to sort and fold laundry but not finishing the task might help you come to an answer?

REFLECTION PAUSE

It was a warm evening in May 2012. I was driving home from my volunteer work helping young people who have committed crimes to turn their lives around. As I drove, I felt a rush of depression come over me. I felt sad. I wanted to stay in that negative energy. But taking my mind to my daily happiness targets helped me to understand that I had completed most of my tasks for that day, which meant that I was closer to overall happiness for that day. Therefore, I was entitled to feel more happy than sad. Somehow, my emotional state changed, and I felt happier.

Think about working on several goals and spread out the activities for achieving those goals each day. To begin, limit yourself to no more than six activities in a day. As you get better at it, you can increase the number. If you start with a lower number of tasks, the more successful you become, the more motivated you will feel to increase your list of goals and daily tasks.

If you are able to complete a daily task earlier in the week than planned, record it on the day it was accomplished. It may mean that your score on that day is higher than projected, which is great. You focus is on the now. You want to achieve your overall weekly target but not go over it.

Strike while the iron is hot! Remember, you can exceed your daily total and record it on your daily monitor, but you cannot exceed your weekly totals. The monitor can only record that you have reached your weekly target. If you are constantly exceeding your weekly targets, then review your goals and revise them, if necessary.

When you build up momentum, you'll find that you are thinking about how you are going to complete outstanding tasks. When you have completed a task, you'll find yourself looking forward to updating your monitor.

Every time you complete the previous period's monitor—that is, you complete your scores for the previous day—consider what you are going to do to complete your tasks now, and in the next moment, and the moment after that, etc.

REACHED DAILY HAPPINESS TARGET

If you reached your target, well done! You now have evidence to confirm that you were continuously happy on this day. Examine the day's activities. Remember what you did, and enjoy that feeling of happiness. You want to feel it again in the next moment.

BELOW YOUR DAILY HAPPINESS TARGET

If you did not reach your target, identify the steps that you were not able to achieve on this day. Understand why you did not meet your target. Will you keep your behavior the same tomorrow? Will you need to modify it in any way?

Unless you have a strong desire to change your activities or score, keep it the same until the end of the month. You will be able to review a full month's data and identify any patterns.

Happiness monitor			Daily monitor							Totals	
Goal	Frequency		Mon	Tue	Wed	Thu	Fri	Sat	Sun		
Health	Daily	X 7	Yes	Yes	Yes	Yes	Yes	Yes	Yes	7	
Totals			1	1	1	1	1	1	1	Actual 7	Target 7

Example of a completed Daily Happiness Goals Monitor

WEEKLY MONITOR

Daily scores will be added up to produce a weekly score. If you reached the weekly happiness target, congratulations! You now have evidence to confirm that you were continuously happy during the week. Review your actions to understand what you did, as you want to keep on behaving in the same way. Review the totals. Were you too severe or too soft on yourself?

It may be possible to achieve your weekly happiness target by exceeding the daily targets on Monday, Tuesday, Wednesday, and Thursday. So, if you are below your targets on Friday, Saturday, and Sunday, you have still achieved your overall weekly score. Review the last week's activities and remember what you did. Enjoy that feeling—happiness. You want to feel it again next week.

Below your weekly happiness target? Identify the days on which you did not meet your target score and see by how much you missed it to understand why. Record the reason that you did not meet your weekly target. Take appropriate action.

Next week, will you keep the target the same or will you need to modify it in some way? Unless you have a strong desire to change your activities or score, keep it the same until the end of the month, when you will be able to review a full month's data and identify any patterns.

PAST PARTICIPANT PROFILE

B is sixty. His sister committed suicide due to poor mental health, and his wife filed for divorce, leaving him with large family debts. He also had to pay child support, and his house was foreclosed. He took voluntary redundancy to help pay off some of the debts. Since 2001, he has accumulated £24,000 (roughly $31,720) worth of debts owed to the council, which include service charge to his home and council tax. He is in a legal dispute with the council over his liability for these debts. He is currently having a dispute with his neighbours over the level of noise they make. Since his divorce, his relationship with his children has broken down. He also has large gambling debts. He is suffering from depression, and his doctor has prescribed medication. After attending the program, his outcomes were that he

- *was able to maintain a relationship with his children and attend all sessions,*
- *had increased social interaction with other members, and*
- *was looking for full-time employment,*

WEEK 1

Happiness monitor	Weekly									Totals
Goal	Frequency		Mon	Tue	Wed	Thu	Fri	Sat	Sun	
Career	Weekly	X1	N/A	N/A	N/A	Yes	N/A	N/A	N/A	1
Financial	Weekly	X1	Yes	N/A	N/A	N/A	N/A	N/A		1
Family	Weekly	X2	N/A	Yes	N/A	N/A	N/A	Yes	N/A	2
Nurture social relationships	Weekly	X6	Yes	Yes	Yes	Yes	Yes	N/A	Yes	6
He alth	Weekly	X7	Yes	Yes	Yes	Yes	Yes	Yes	Yes	7
Exercise	Weekly	X4	N/A	N/A	Yes	Yes	Yes	Yes	N/A	4
Gratitude : Say Thank You Like You Mean It	Weekly	X6	Yes	Yes	N/A	Yes	Yes	Yes	Yes	6
Smile Even When You Don't Feel Like It	Weekly	X6	Yes	Yes	Yes	Yes	N/A	Yes	Yes	6
spirituality, Pray & Meditate	Weekly	X1	N/A	N/A	Yes	N/A	N/A	N/A	N/A	1
Play and have fun	Weekly	X2	N/A	N/A	Yes	N/A	N/A	N/A	Yes	2
Target score	Weekly	36	5	5	6	5	5	5	5	36
Actual score	Weekly	36	5	5	6	5	5	5	5	36
Difference + or −	Weekly	0	0	0	0	0	0	0	0	-
Comments										

Example of a completed weekly happiness goals monitor, week 1

How to use Feeling Very Good as a way into the Happiness Zone

WEEK 2

Happiness monitor	Weekly									Totals
Goal	Frequency		Mon	Tue	Wed	Thu	Fri	Sat	Sun	
Career	Weekly	X1	N/A	N/A	N/A	N/A	Yes	N/A	N/A	1
Financial	Weekly	X1	Yes	N/A	N/A	N/A	N/A	N/A		1
Family	Weekly	X2	N/A	Yes	N/A	N/A	N/A	Yes	N/A	2
Nurture social relationships	Weekly	X6	Yes	Yes	Yes	Yes	Yes	N/A	Yes	6
He alth	Weekly	X7	Yes	Yes	Yes	Yes	Yes	Yes	Yes	7
Exercise	Weekly	X4	N/A	N/A	Yes	Yes	Yes	Yes	N/A	4
Gratitude : Say Thank You Like You Mean It	Weekly	X6	Yes	Yes	N/A	Yes	Yes	Yes	Yes	6
Smile Even When You Don't Feel Like It	Weekly	X6	Yes	Yes	Yes	Yes	N/A	Yes	Yes	6
spirituality, Pray & Meditate	Weekly	X1	N/A	N/A	Yes	N/A	N/A	N/A	N/A	1
Play and have fun	Weekly	X2	N/A	N/A	Yes	N/A	N/A	N/A	Yes	2
Target score	Weekly	36	5	5	6	5	5	5	5	36
Actual score	Weekly	36	5	5	6	5	5	5	5	36
Difference + or −	Weekly	0	0	0	0	0	0	0	0	-
Comments										

Example of a completed weekly happiness goals monitor, week 2

WEEK 3

Happiness monitor			Weekly							Totals
Goal	Frequency		Mon	Tue	Wed	Thu	Fri	Sat	Sun	
Career	Weekly	X1	N/A	N/A	N/A	N/A	Yes	N/A	N/A	1
Financial	Weekly	X1	Yes	N/A	N/A	N/A	N/A	N/A		1
Family	Weekly	X2	N/A	Yes	N/A	N/A	N/A	Yes	N/A	2
Nurture social relationships	Weekly	X6	Yes	Yes	Yes	Yes	Yes	N/A	Yes	6
He alth	Weekly	X7	Yes	Yes	Yes	Yes	Yes	Yes	Yes	7
Exercise	Weekly	X4	N/A	N/A	Yes	Yes	Yes	Yes	N/A	4
Gratitude : Say Thank You Like You Mean It	Weekly	X6	Yes	Yes	N/A	Yes	Yes	Yes	Yes	6
Smile Even When You Don't Feel Like It	Weekly	X6	Yes	Yes	Yes	Yes	N/A	Yes	Yes	6
spirituality, Pray & Meditate	Weekly	X1	N/A	N/A	Yes	N/A	N/A	N/A	N/A	1
Play and have fun	Weekly	X2	N/A	N/A	Yes	N/A	N/A	N/A	Yes	2
Target score	Weekly	36	5	5	6	5	5	5	5	36
Actual score	Weekly	36	5	5	6	5	5	5	5	36
Difference + or −	Weekly	0	0	0	0	0	0	0	0	-
Comments										

Example of a completed weekly happiness goals monitor, week 3

How to use Feeling Very Good as a way into the Happiness Zone

WEEK 4

Happiness monitor	Weekly									Totals
Goal	Frequency		Mon	Tue	Wed	Thu	Fri	Sat	Sun	
Career	Weekly	X1	N/A	N/A	N/A	N/A	Yes	N/A	N/A	1
Financial	Weekly	X1	Yes	N/A	N/A	N/A	N/A	N/A		1
Family	Weekly	X2	N/A	Yes	N/A	N/A	N/A	Yes	N/A	2
Nurture social relationships	Weekly	X6	Yes	Yes	Yes	Yes	Yes	N/A	Yes	6
He alth	Weekly	X7	Yes	Yes	Yes	Yes	Yes	Yes	Yes	7
Exercise	Weekly	X4	N/A	N/A	Yes	Yes	Yes	Yes	N/A	4
Gratitude : Say Thank You Like You Mean It	Weekly	X6	Yes	Yes	N/A	Yes	Yes	Yes	Yes	6
Smile Even When You Don't Feel Like It	Weekly	X6	Yes	Yes	Yes	Yes	N/A	Yes	Yes	6
spirituality, Pray & Meditate	Weekly	X1	N/A	N/A	Yes	N/A	N/A	N/A	N/A	1
Play and have fun	Weekly	X2	N/A	N/A	Yes	N/A	N/A	N/A	Yes	2
Target score	Weekly	36	5	5	6	5	5	5	5	36
Actual score	Weekly	36	5	5	6	5	5	5	5	36
Difference + or –	Weekly	0	0	0	0	0	0	0	0	-
Comments										

Example of a completed weekly happiness goals monitor, week 4

WEEK 5

In week 5, you notice that you did not undertake your exercise on Wednesday because you had to work overtime and arrived home too late. If this is a one-off, you can intend to make up the extra session within the week. However, if you find that you regularly have to work late, you may have to reduce the number of times you schedule exercise or change it to another day of the week.

Happiness monitor	Daily/Weekly									Totals
Goal	Frequency		Mon	Tue	Wed	Thu	Fri	Sat	Sun	
Career	Weekly	X1	N/A	N/A	N/A	N/A	Yes	N/A	N/A	1
Financial	Weekly	X1	Yes	N/A	N/A	N/A	N/A	N/A		1
Family	Weekly	X2	N/A	Yes	N/A	N/A	N/A	Yes	N/A	2
Nurture social relationships	Weekly	X6	Yes	Yes	Yes	Yes	Yes	N/A	Yes	6
Health	Weekly	X7	Yes	Yes	Yes	Yes	Yes	Yes	Yes	7
Exercise	Weekly	X4	N/A	N/A	No	Yes	Yes	Yes	N/A	3
Gratitude: Say Thank You Like You Mean It	Weekly	X6	Yes	Yes	N/A	Yes	Yes	Yes	Yes	6
Smile Even When You Don't Feel Like It	Weekly	X6	Yes	Yes	Yes	Yes	N/A	Yes	Yes	6
spirituality, Pray & Meditate	Weekly	X1	N/A	N/A	Yes	N/A	N/A	N/A	N/A	1
Play and have fun	Weekly	X2	N/A	N/A	Yes	N/A	N/A	N/A	Yes	2
Target score	Weekly		36	5	5	6	5	5	5	5	36
Actual score	Weekly		35	5	5	5	5	5	5	5	35
Difference + or −	Weekly		-1	0	0	-1	0	0	0	0	-1
Comments: No exercise on Wednesday due to overtime at work and got home late.										

Example of a completed weekly happiness goals monitor, week 5

MONTHLY MONITOR

Weekly scores will be added up to create a monthly score. Add monthly scores to the monthly monitor, so you can track them. See below. If you reached your monthly target, congratulations! You now have evidence to confirm that you were continuously happy during the month.

Review the totals. Were you too severe or too soft on yourself? Review the last month's activities and remember what you did. Enjoy that feeling—happiness. You want to feel it again next month.

If you were below your monthly happiness target, identify the weeks that you did not meet your target. Understand why and record the reasons. You can now decide if you want to change or modify a goal or the activities to achieve an objective.

Next month, will you keep the target the same or will you need to modify it in any way? Unless you have a strong desire to change your activities or score, keep it the same until the end of the month. You then will be able to review another full month's data and identify any patterns.

MONTH 1

Toward the end of the first month, you will find that you are closing the gap between your target score and your actual score. In some cases, you will reach and maintain your target score. The next step is to keep it up the following month.

If you have not reached your target score by the end of the month, you must review your scores on a weekly and, if necessarily, a daily basis to understand where you are falling short. You have to take action to amend your behavior to work on ensuring that your target and actual scores are the same.

MONTHLY MONITOR

Monthly happiness monitor	Monthly					Totals
	Week 1 Date:	Week 2 Date:	Week 3 Date:	Week 4 Date:	Week 5 Date:	
Career	1	1	1	1	1	5
Financial	1	1	1	1	1	5
Family	2	2	2	2	2	10
Nurture social relationships	6	6	6	6	6	30
Health	7	7	7	7	7	35
Exercise	4	4	4	4	3	19
Gratitude Say Thank You Like You Mean It	6	6	6	6	6	30
Smile Even When You Don't Feel Like It	6	6	6	6	6	30
spirituality, Pray & Meditate	1	1	1	1	1	5
Play and have fun	2	2	2	2	2	10
Target happy score	36	36	36	36	36	180
Actual happy score	36	36	36	36	35	179
Difference + or -					-1	-1
Comments: Did not meet monthly target because no exercise on Wednesdays due to overtime at work and getting home late.						

Example of a completed monthly happiness goals monitor

YEARLY MONITOR

Add up monthly scores to produce a yearly score and add it to the yearly monitor, as shown below. Did you reach the yearly target?

If yes, well done! Review your actions to understand what you did as you want to carry on that behaviour. If no, by how much were you off? You need to understand why you're not achieving your target score. Work out what you wanted to do, what you actually did, and understand why there was a difference between the two. Decide how you will change next time.

Once you have identified that you are regularly reaching your target score overall, celebrate!

Happiness Monitor					Yearly							
Goals	1	2	3	4	5	6	7	8	9	10	11	12
Career	5	5	5	5	5	5	5	5	5	5	5	5
Financial	5	5	5	5	5	5	5	5	5	5	5	5
Family	10	10	10	10	10	10	10	10	10	10	10	10
Nurture social relationships	30	30	30	30	30	30	30	30	30	30	30	30
Health	35	35	35	35	35	35	35	35	35	35	35	35
Exercise	19	19	19	19	19	19	19	19	19	19	19	19
Gratitude Say Thank You Like You Mean It	30	30	30	30	30	30	30	30	30	30	30	30
Smile Even When You Don't Feel Like It	30	30	30	30	30	30	30	30	30	30	30	30
spirituality, Pray & Meditate	5	5	5	5	5	5	5	5	5	5	5	5
Play and have fun	10	10	10	10	10	10	10	10	10	10	10	10
Actual happy score	179	179	179	179	179	179	179	179	179	179	179	179
Target happy score	180	180	180	180	180	180	180	180	180	180	180	180
Difference	-1	-1	-1	-1	-1	-1	-1	-1	-1	-1	-1	-1
Comments: Did not meet yearly target because no exercise on Wednesdays due to overtime at work and getting home late.												

Example of a completed yearly happiness goals monitor

6

Adjustment to the Happiness Goals Monitor

This chapter explains the factors involved in making the relevant adjustments to your monitor after reviewing and evaluating it. Have you met your target score in a given period? Is there any need to adjust your monitor?

DAILY/WEEKLY ADJUSTMENT TO THE HAPPINESS GOAL MONITOR

Use the daily/weekly adjustment form (page 47) to understand if any adjustments need to be made to your Happiness Monitor. After each week, you will begin to see a performance pattern in relation to your target score and your actual score.

OVER PERFORMING

If you find that you are exceeding your score, you need to understand why. Based on the reason, you might want to

- remove the goal because you have achieved it,
- revise the goal to be a little more challenging, or
- make a new goal to be a little more challenging.

MEETING YOUR TARGET

If you are regularly reaching your target score but have not yet completed the goal, there is no need for further action. You just need to continue to monitor the situation.

As soon as you achieve a goal, remove the tasks associated with that goal from your daily list and just focus on the goals that you have not yet met. By working on fewer goals at any one time, you are able to concentrate your energies; it is also less stressful.

PAST PARTICIPANT PROFILE

M is fifty-three. She is married with five children and has kidney failure. She has to go for dialysis treatment three times each week and cannot stand for long periods of time. After attending the program, her outcomes were that she

- *was able to maintain regular attendance,*
- *engaged with other members of the group, and*
- *undertook computer training to identify if that was a possible career avenue.*

NOT MEETING YOUR TARGET

If you have not met your target score, you will be able to identify what you planned to do and what you actually did from your daily/weekly monitoring sheet.

The monitoring sheet has a comments box for you to record the reasons for the action. It's important to complete the box at the end of each period, while the details are fresh in your mind. This will provide important information in the future to identify any patterns that are emerging.

The question that you must ask yourself is, "How will I change my actions in the next monitoring period to reach my target score?"

The one person I recommend that you are honest with is yourself! As you work toward completing the steps that will take you closer to your goal, it is wise to be realistic with yourself. If you find that you are regularly not achieving your target score, change the activities or accept that you will never reach those goals and remove or amend them. If you do not know how to change your action in a certain area, your first step could be to find out how to change your behavior. The key is that if you are not getting the results that you want or expect, then do something different.

WEEK 5

In week 5 of the sample Happiness Monitor, exercise was not completed on a particular day. On Wednesday, you had to work overtime and arrived home too late for a workout. If this is a one-off, you can make up the extra session within the week. However, if you find that you regularly having to work late, you may have to reduce the number of times you exercise or change your workout to another day of the week.

Areas to work on	What did you intend to do	What did you do this period	What are you going to do different next period, is it SMART (specific, measurable, achievable, realistic and timed).
Exercise	Go to the gym on Wednesdays	Overtime at work; therefore could not go.	This is outside my control. If I have to continue to do overtime on Wednesdays. I will have to reduce the numbers of days I go to the gym or go on a different time or day.

Example of monitoring, evaluating, and adjusting the happiness goal monitor

MONTHLY ADJUSTMENT TO THE HAPPINESS GOAL MONITOR

Use the monthly adjustment form (appendix 13) to understand if any adjustments need to be made to your Happiness Monitor. After each month, you will begin to see a performance pattern in relation to your target score and your actual score.

YEARLY ADJUSTMENT TO THE HAPPINESS GOAL MONITOR

Use the yearly adjustment form (appendix 14) to understand if any adjustments needs to be made to your yearly Happiness Monitor. After each year, you will begin to see a performance pattern in relation to your target score and your actual score.

After twelve months, you will have a complete picture of your activities over the year. You can remove goals that have been achieved or ones you no longer want to work toward from the Happiness Monitor.

REFLECTION PAUSE

There was one notable exception when I first started to deliver the program. I had very little money and a recycling operation said I could use its training room for free. It was a little scruffy, with bars on the window, and one of the program participants was an ex-offender. He said that having the bars on the window reminded him of prison, and he found it depressing. He did not feel very happy in the surroundings.

The following week, I changed the venue to a pleasant, open-plan room. Unfortunately, that particular participant never returned and did not benefit from the fact that his comment had been taken on board, and the venue was changed. Since that experience, whenever possible I am extremely careful in the choice of venue to deliver happy training sessions.

7

Conclusion

Happiness, which is another word for contentment, can be described as choosing to do whatever you want, without hurting anyone or breaking any laws. Different people define happiness in different ways.

I believe that you can be happy by focusing on what makes you feel good. You will immediately start to feel the benefits of this approach by using the Happiness Monitor.

Regularly reviewing the steps that you have to take to reach your goals will give you a feeling of well-being. To feel continuous happiness, which is contentment, choose to regularly update your Lifetime Happiness Plan to stay in the Happiness Zone.

REFLECTION PAUSE
I believe that the only person you have to be honest with is yourself!

8

Appendix

APPENDIX 1: CONTENTMENT

Contentment begins when what you have is the same or more than what you need or desire. Or when you stay in the Happiness Zone when something is good or not so good.

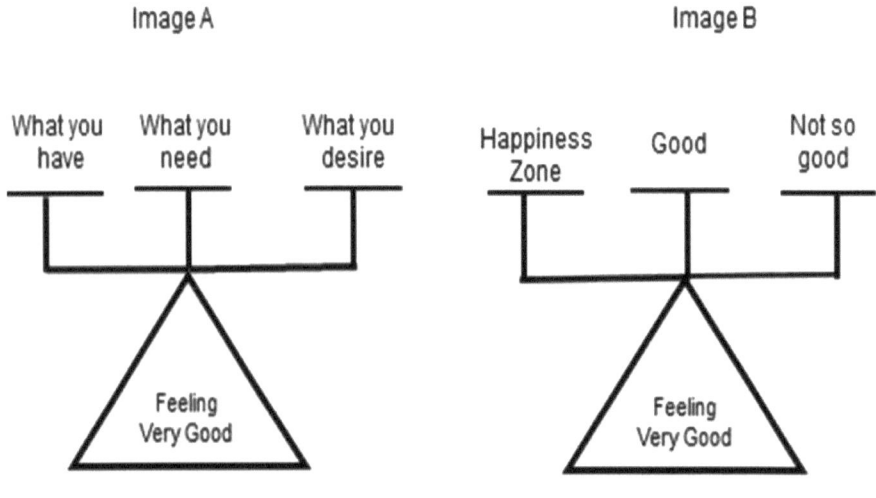

APPENDIX 2: MASLOW'S HIERARCHY OF NEEDS

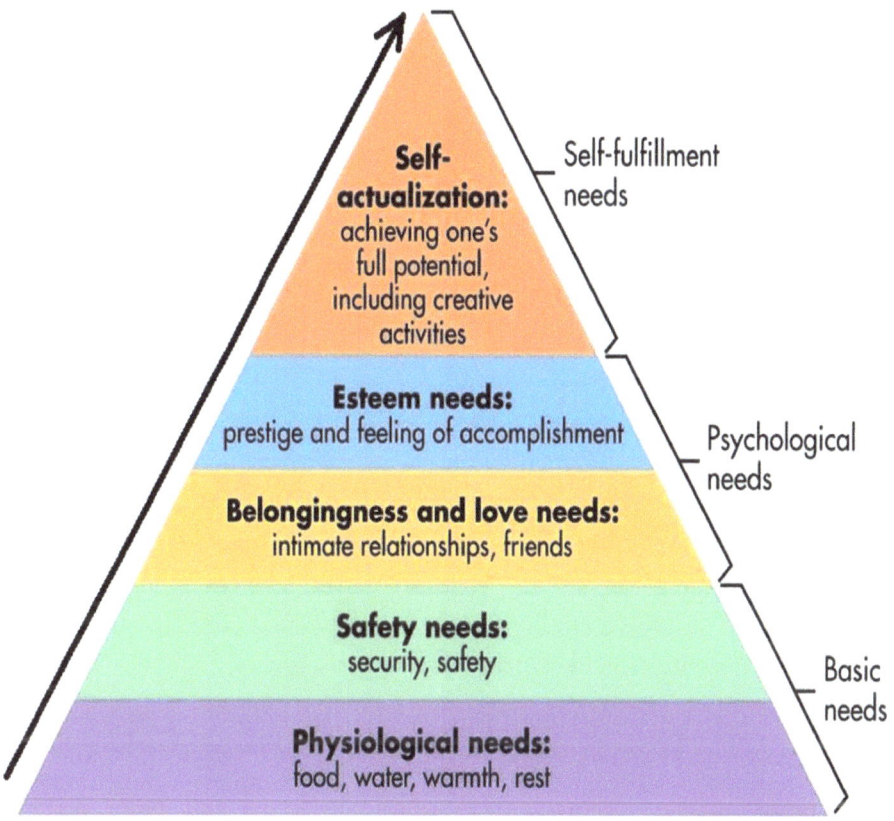

MASLOW'S HIERARCHY OF NEEDS

The original five-stage model of the hierarchy of needs includes the following needs:

1. Physiological needs—breathing, food, drink, shelter, warmth, sex, sleep, homeostasis, bowel movements—that is, basic health needs.
2. Safety needs—protection from elements (income from employment), security of body (home), order, law, stability, freedom from fear, etc.
3. Love and belongingness needs—friendship, intimacy, trust, acceptance, receiving and giving affection and love, affiliating, being part of a group (family, friends, or work), etc.
4. Esteem or psychological needs—self-esteem, confidence, achievement, mastery, independence, status, dominance, prestige, self-respect, and respect from others (e.g., managerial responsibility), etc.
5. Self-actualization or self-fulfillment needs—realizing personal potential, morality, creativity, spontaneity, problem solving, lack of prejudice, acceptance of facts, self-fulfillment, personal growth, and seeking of peak experiences, etc.

Note that although Maslow referred to additional aspects of motivation—cognitive, aesthetic, and transcendence—he did not include any of these as additional stages in the hierarchy of needs.

This five-stage model can be divided into deficiency needs and growth needs. The first four levels are often referred to as deficiency needs (D needs) and the top level comprises growth or being needs (B needs). The deficiency needs are said to motivate people when they are unmet. Also, the need to fulfill such needs will become stronger the longer they are denied. For example, the longer a person goes without food, the hungrier he or she will become.

One must satisfy lower-level deficit needs before progressing to meet higher-level growth needs. When a deficit need has been satisfied, it will go away. Our activities become habitually directed toward meeting the next set of needs that we have yet to satisfy. These then become our salient needs. However, growth needs continue to be felt and may even become stronger once they have been engaged.

EXAMPLES IN USE

You can't motivate someone to achieve his sales target (level 4) when he's having problems with his marriage (level 3). You can't expect someone to work as a team member (level 3) when her house is being repossessed (level 2). Once these growths needs have been reasonably satisfied, one may be able to reach the highest level, which is called self-actualization.

Every person is capable and has the desire to move up the hierarchy toward a level of self-actualization. Unfortunately, progress is often disrupted by failure to meet lower-level needs. Life experiences, including divorce and loss of job, may cause an individual to fluctuate between levels of the hierarchy. Therefore, not everyone will move through the hierarchy in a unidirectional manner. Some may move back and forth between the different types of needs. Maslow noted that only one in a hundred people become fully self-actualized because our society rewards motivation primarily based on esteem, love, and other social needs.

CHARACTERISTICS OF SELF-ACTUALIZED PEOPLE

Although we are all theoretically capable of self-actualizing, most of us will not do so—or we will only do so to a limited degree. Maslow estimated that only 2 percent of people will reach the state of self-actualization. He was particularly interested in the characteristics of people whom he considered to have achieved their potential as persons.

By studying eighteen people he considered to be self-actualized (including Abraham Lincoln and Albert Einstein), in *Motivation and Personality*, Maslow identified fifteen characteristics of the self-actualized person. They include the following:

1. They perceive reality efficiently and can tolerate uncertainty.
2. They accept themselves and others for what they are.

3. They are spontaneous in thought and action.
4. They are problem-centered (not self-centered).
5. They have unusual senses of humor.
6. They are able to look at life objectively.
7. They are highly creative.
8. They are resistant to enculturation but not purposely unconventional.
9. They are concerned for the welfare of humanity.
10. They are capable of deep appreciation of basic life experience.
11. They establish deep, satisfying interpersonal relationships with a few people.
12. They have peak experiences.
13. They have a need for privacy.
14. They hold democratic attitudes.
15. They have strong moral/ethical standards.

According to Maslow, behaviors leading to self-actualization include the following:

- experiencing life like a child, with full absorption and concentration
- trying new things instead of sticking to safe paths
- listening to your own feelings in evaluating experiences instead of to the voice of tradition, authority, or the majority
- avoiding pretense ("game playing") and being honest
- being prepared to be unpopular if your views do not coincide with those of the majority
- taking responsibility and working hard
- trying to identify your defenses and having the courage to give them up

The characteristics of self-actualizers and the behaviours leading to self-actualization are shown in the lists above. Although people achieve self-actualization in their own unique ways, they tend to share certain characteristics. However, self-actualization is a matter of degree. "There are no perfect human beings," Maslow said.

It is not necessary to display all fifteen characteristics to become self-actualized, and not only self-actualized people will display them. Maslow did not equate self-actualization with perfection. Self-actualization merely involves achieving one's potential. Thus, someone can be silly, wasteful, vain, and impolite and still self-actualize.

APPENDIX 3: LIFETIME HAPPINESS PLAN 1

	Lifetime Happiness Plan:- Contentment, page 1 of 2 Express using your five main senses: Sight, Hearing, Taste, Smell, and Touch.		
Name:		Signature:	Date:
Time line	Feel Very Good goals	Needs goals Basic, Psychological, and Self-fulfilment	Desire goals Mind, Body and Soul/Sprit
Within 6 months			
Within in a year			
Beyond			

How to use Feeling Very Good as a way into the Happiness Zone

LIFETIME HAPPINESS PLAN 2

Lifetime Happiness Plan:- Contentment, page 2 of 2
Express using your five main senses: Sight, Hearing, Taste, Smell, and Touch.

Name: Signature: Date:

APPENDIX 4: CONTENTMENT GOALS LIST

Contentment goals list	Goals target achievement date	Goals target weekly activities	Goals target daily engagement duration

APPENDIX 5: HAPPY SMART GOAL-SETTING SHEET 1 OF 7

SMART Happiness goal sheet page 1 of 7	
Overall aim:	
Goal:	
Specific:	
Who	
When	
Where	
Why	

SMART Happiness specific steps measurable sheet, page 2 of 7	
Name:	Date:
Specific what are you going to do:	
List actions:	How will you measure results?
List results and any changes in your environment	

Attainable/
Achievable,
page 3 of 7

Realistic/
Relevant,
page 4 of 7

How to use Feeling Very Good as a way into the Happiness Zone

Time/
By When,
page 5 of 7

SMART Happiness Goal Barriers, page 6 of 7	
Goal:	
Barriers	Overcome Barriers

SMART Happiness Goal Help, page 7 of 7	
Goal:	
Help	Work on Help

APPENDIX 6: EDWARD DE BONO'S SIX THINKING HATS

Individuals and organizations want to be creative and develop ideas that effectively address pressing issues and opportunities. Edward De Bono developed the Six Thinking Hats and published his parallel-thinking concepts in 1985.

THINKING HAT 1

Coloured Hat	Deal with	Questions
	Blue Hat is process control "thinking about thinking". This is the hat worn by people chairing or facilitating the session. Blue Hat may be used at the beginning of the session to set the agenda or the sequence for using the "hats" and at the end of the session when seeking a summary and next step. Blue Hat focuses on questioning (fishing and shooting – p.153) and provides the structure for use of other hats and other thinking/problem-solving tools	Define the Issue and Process What is the problem? Is this the real problem? What is the underlying problem? Why do we need to solve this problem? Where should we go first? Where do we start? What should we be thinking about? Assessment of the Process Are we getting anywhere? What factors should we consider? What sort of outcome would we regard as successful? What have we achieved so far? Management/Facilitation Could you put on the "X" hat? You're not using the "X" hat.

How to use Feeling Very Good as a way into the Happiness Zone

THINKING HATS 2

Coloured Hat	Deal with	Questions
	White Hat focuses on available data (facts and figures) while remaining neutral. Participants are encouraged to review existing information, search for gaps in knowledge, analyse past trends, and extrapolate key learnings from historical data.	What inform ation do we have? What information do we need? What information is mission? What questions do we need to ask? How are we going to get the information we need? Is it fact or belief?
	Red Hat uses intuition, gut reaction, and robust emotion. En courages participants to think about how other people will react emotionally and try to understand the responses of people who do not fully know your reasoning. Participants do not need to explain or justify individual expressions of feelings	How do you re act to this? What is your intuition/opinion about this? Gut feelings .. .Hunches or insights . . .Likes/dislikes? What emotions [fear, anger, hatred, suspicion, jealousy, or love (53)] are involved here?
	Yellow Hat is a deliberate search fo r the positive (optimistic viewpoint) through exploration and speculation defining the benefits of the decision and the value in it. Yellow Hat thinking is constructive blending "curiosity, pleasure, greed, and the desire to make things happen" (91) enhanc ing the proposal by generating alternative ideas "based on experience, available information, logical	What ideas, suggestions, or proposals are there for how to approach this problem? . . .to achieve this goal? What is the merit of the approach? What positives can you see in this idea? What could be done to make this work better? Faster? More economically? Under what conditions could this work? What would it take to make this proposal acceptable? What is y our vision for how this could

THINKING HATS 3

Coloured Hat	Deal with	Questions
	Green Hat stands for energy and creativity. This is where you generate new, innovative ideas and develop creative solutions to a problem. It is freewheeling way of thinking in which there is little criticism of ideas, and "movement" is made using provocation to move "forward with an idea or from an idea" (125) seeking alternative solutions. Green Hat thinking must involve shaping the idea for the user or "buyer".	Let's think "outside the box." What are some fresh ideas or approaches? This is the time for any wild or crazy or "far out" idea. What are all of our alternatives here? Aren't there some other alternatives . . . perhaps too outside the box? This idea won't work in its present form, but can we shape it or adapt it so that it might be usable? We've always done it this way; let's "green hat" it .. .does it have to be done this way?
	Black Hat is the basis of logical, critical thinking offering careful, cautious, and defensive insights. Try to see what is wrong; why it might not work; what are the dangers, problems, and obstacles; what the deficiencies are in the thinking process. It allows you to eliminate the negatives, alter plans, or prepare contingency plans to counter any problems. Black Hat thinking is not an argument, but helps to make plans "tougher" and more resilient. It can help to spot fatal flaws and risks before you embark on a course of action. There is a danger of overusing black hat thinking by remaining in the critical mode and delaying green and yellow hat thinking.	What will happen if we take this action? What can go wrong if we proceed with this idea or implement this suggestion? What are the weaknesses that we need to overcome? How does this "fit" with our (or other's) experience, policy, strategy, values, ethics, and resources? How will people respond? Will it work .. be profitable .. be acceptable?

APPENDIX 7: TESTIMONIALS FROM PAST PARTICIPANTS

This section contains a selection of feedback from past participants in the program.

"I was going to buy a bottle of scotch, then I remembered that I was going to the session, and that stopped me from drinking." (A recovering alcoholic)

"After attending the program, I don't feel so depressed."

"I feel more positive about the future now."

"I can now see a good future."

"I have a lot more confidence, in general, now."

"When I have a problem, I remember the saying I learned from the course: just because I had a setback, it doesn't mean I have to stay back."

"The program has given me coping strategies."

"I now feel more courageous."

"Never lose hope."

"I approach situations and problems in different ways and come out of my comfort zone—do things differently."

"Never give up!"

"I'll try to motivate myself."

"Continue to practice and change if something is not working."

"Improve my interview techniques and also stick to the goal planner, which I learned."

"I am going to implement everything learned from training continuously."

"I hope to apply the SMART procedures in my future planning."

"This program helped me to set goals and think outside the box; very happy to have attended the program."

"Maintain it."

"It helped to give me a different perspective."

"It was a good training and well interactive, and I enjoyed being with everyone that was involved in the training."

"I am going to practice SMART goal setting."

"I am going to use my Lifetime Happiness plan and Happiness Bank especially, which is very helpful!"

"I will always think positively."

"Forget about the 'why' and carry on focusing on me, what I control and what I can influence, as the focusing on the 'why' makes me frustrated and annoyed."

"Think differently after doing this course. Path is more clear and how to achieve it."

"Make my goals SMART."

"I really enjoyed this course and meeting people. Everyone was really friendly, and I interacted well with them. Gil was very friendly, welcoming, and down to earth!"

"Strongly recommend this to all."

"I would recommend to my friend."

"I am going to apply what I have learned in this course to all aspects of my life, in particular, goal setting. This course has made me feel more confident in achieving my aims."

"I am going to do regular exercise to bring more motivation into my life…"

"A very valuable and worthwhile course; for the future, I'm now Feeling Very Good."

"I will be better, confident, and more challenging and effective."

"I can now look ahead and think more constructively."

You can see filmed testimonials by going to: https://www.youtube.com/channel/UCzdPFYgFqXesMVJfe0BqmcA

APPENDIX 8: AUTHOR BIOGRAPHY

Gilbert George Pennant Junior is the creator of the **Getting into the Happiness Zone: Setting Goals for Success** program, a motivational and empowering goal-setting course that can be followed with one-to-one support sessions. The course, which has been delivered to the public, private, and voluntary sectors, gives each person a Lifetime Happiness Action plan. The program uses **feelings** as a way of increasing happiness and well-being and uses mindfulness to help people move forward with their lives.

Gilbert is the originator of Gilism, an approach to life that focuses on feelings as a way into the Happiness Zone, the contentment of having at least what you need or desire. A range of inspirational posters are for sale at www.feelingvg.com and #gilism.

Gilbert is an accomplished and experienced trainer and brings a fresh, thought-provoking, interactive and innovative approach to his training courses. He has a diploma in management, a diploma in the arts and science of neuro-linguistic programming, Prince 2 project management qualifications He is also a qualified chair-based exercise instructor.

Gilbert is a management consultant (one of his specialities being traded services) and has worked for over twenty years in the public, private, and charity sectors. He has used this experience about the world of work to develop the 'Manage Yourself to be Valuable in the Workplace' program.

Gilbert is also a volunteer on youth offender panels and other court work, and he serves a community mediator.

How to Use Feeling as a Way into the Happiness Zone is his second publication. He is also the author of *Grapevine: A Directory of African Caribbean Community Groups in the UK.*

For more information, go to the Gil Pennant channel on YouTube or #gilpennant. Or e-mail at gil.pennant@gmail.com.

APPENDIX 9: DAILY/WEEKLY HAPPINESS GOALS MONITOR

Happiness monitor		Daily/Weekly							Totals
Goal	Frequency	Mon	Tue	Wed	Thu	Fri	Sat	Sun	
Target score									
Actual score									
Difference									
Comments:									

APPENDIX 10: MONTHLY HAPPINESS GOALS MONITOR

Monthly happiness monitor	Monthly					Totals
	Week 1 Date:	Week 2 Date:	Week 3 Date:	Week 4 Date:	Week 5 Date:	
Target happy score						
Actual happy score						
Difference + or -						
Comments:						

APPENDIX 11: YEARLY HAPPINESS GOALS MONITOR

Happiness Monitor							Yearly					
Goals	1	2	3	4	5	6	7	8	9	10	11	12
Actual happy score												
Target happy score												
Difference												
Comments:												

APPENDIX 12: WEEKLY HAPPINESS GOALS ADJUSTMENT MONITOR

Weekly happiness goals adjustment monitor			
Goals to work on	What did you intend to do	What did you do this period	What are you going to do different next period, is it SMART (specific, measurable, achievable, realistic and timed).

APPENDIX 13: MONTHLY HAPPINESS GOALS ADJUSTMENT MONITOR

Monthly happiness goals adjustment monitor			
Goals to work on	What did you intend to do	What did you do this period	What are you going to do different next period, is it SMART (specific, measurable, achievable, realistic and timed).

APPENDIX 14: YEARLY HAPPINESS GOALS ADJUSTMENT MONITOR

Yearly happiness goals adjustment monitor			
Goals to work on	What did you intend to do	What did you do this period	What are you going to do different next period, is it SMART (specific, measurable, achievable, realistic and timed).

APPENDIX 15: GLOSSARY

FEELING VERY GOOD SAVINGS ACCOUNT
You deposit anything that makes you feel good—good memories, past success, music, gratitude, etc.

GILISM
An approach to life that focuses on feelings as a way into the Happiness Zone. In the Happiness Zone, contentment is when what you have is the same or more than what you need or desire.

HAPPINESS BANK
The Happiness Bank is where you open your Feeling Very Good savings account. You deposit anything that makes you feel good—good memories, past success, music, gratitude, etc.

HAPPINESS ZONE
This is where you are able to focus on something that makes you feel very good in order to create the life you want. It's also the ability to remain in the same positive frame of mind when things are good and when they are not so good.

LIFETIME HAPPINESS PLAN
The Lifetime Happiness Plan is a document that helps you think about, visualize, and actualize all of the pieces that make up your picture of happiness, which is contentment. It's divided into three sets of goals: Feeling Very Good goals, Needs goals, and What You Desire goals. It helps you to set out the direction, priorities, goals, and time frame to go forward with your plan.

LIFE-LIFE BALANCE
Work is important but does not represent 50 percent of your existence. Therefore, by using the Lifetime Happiness Plan, you divide life into three

areas with three sets of goals: Feeling Very Good goals, Needs goals, and What You Desire goals.

SMART HAPPY GOALS

A "happy" goal sets out the steps to be taken to achieve an aim. The more detail you can include in each of the steps on your journey, the better the chance of success. The purpose of a range of goals is to contribute to an overall objective, which, in the Happiness Zone, is to reach a feeling of contentment. A SMART goal is one obtained by actions that are all specific, measurable, achievable, realistic/relevant, and timed.

APPENDIX 16: BIBLIOGRAPHY

- Boehm, J. K. and S. Lyubomirsky. "Does Happiness Promote Career Success?" *Journal of Career Assessment* 16, no. 1 (2008): 101–116.
- Cloninger, C. Robert. *Feeling Good: The Science of Well-Being*. Oxford: Oxford University Press, 2004.
- De Bono, Edward. *Six Thinking Hats*. Boston: Little, Brown & Co., 1985.
- DeMesa, Jimmy M.D. *Be Happy! Your Guide to the Happiest Possible Life*. Sanford, Florida: DC Press, 2006.
- Gentry, W. Doyle. *Happiness for Dummies*. Hoboken, New Jersey: Wiley, 2008.
- Gilbert, Daniel. *Stumbling on Happiness*. New York: Knopf, 2006.
- Graham, Carol. *Happiness around the World: The Paradox of Happy Peasants and Miserable Millionaires*. Oxford: Oxford University Press, 2010.
- Hills, P., and M. Argyle. "The Oxford Happiness Questionnaire: A Compact Scale for the Measurement of Psychological Well-Being." *Personality and Individual Differences* 33, no. 7 (2002): 1,073–1,082.
- Kipfer, Barbara Ann. *14,000 Things to Be Happy About*. New York: Workman Publishing, 1990.
- Klein, Stefan. *The Science of Happiness*. Boston: De Capo Press, 2006.
- Koenig, H.G., M. McCullough, and D.B. Larson. *Handbook of Religion and Health: A Century of Research Reviewed*. New York: Oxford University Press, 2001.
- Layard, Richard. *Happiness*. New York: Penguin Book Group, 2005.
- Layard, Richard. *Happiness: Lessons from a New Science*. London: Penguin, 2005.
- Lyubomirsky, Sonja. *The How of Happiness*. New York: Penguin Group, 2007.

- Maslow, A. H. "A Theory of Human Motivation." Classics in the History of Psychology. Accessed November 19, 2017. http://psychclassics.yorku.ca/Maslow/motivation.htm.
- Maslow, A. H., *Motivation and Personality*. London: Longman, 1970.
- McMahon, Darrin M. *Happiness: A History*. New York: Atlantic Monthly Press, 2005.
- McMahon, Darrin M. "The History of Happiness: 400 B.C.–A.D. 1780." *Daedalus* 133, no. 2 (2004): 5–17.
- Morris, Desmond. The Nature of Happiness, Saginaw, Michigan: Little Books, 2004.
- Myers, David G. *The Pursuit of Happiness*. New York: William Morrow and Co., 1992.
- Richard Bandler, Co-Developer of NLP. "About Richard." Accessed November 17, 2017. www.richardbandler.com.
- Seligman, Martin E.P. *Authentic Happiness*, New York: Atria Books, 2004.
- Sgroi, Daniel, Thomas Hills, Gus O'Donnell, Andrew Oswald, and Eugenio Proto. "Understanding Happiness." Centre for Competitive Advantage in the Global Economy, University of Warwick. Accessed November 19, 2017. https://www.andrewoswald.com/docs/HappinessReport2017V1.pdf.
- Wilson, Eric G. *Against Happiness*. New York: Farrar, Straus & Giroux, 2008.
- Władysław, Tatarkiewicz. *Analysis of Happiness*, The Hague: MartinusNijhoff Publishers, 1976.

APPENDIX 17 LEARNING OBJECTIVES FOR ANYONE READING THIS BOOK

- To understand what makes you feel good.
- To understand what a goal is and why goal setting is important.
- How to set a SMART goal.
- A tool kit to set up a lifetime happiness plan for 1 year, 5 years and beyond.
- A method to set up a happiness goals monitor.
- An approach to monitor, evaluate and adjust a forward happiness plan.
- A focus and clear direction.
- An action plan for a specific period of time going forward.
- Help to visualize and plan actions to achieve goals and the steps to carry them out.
- Improved self-image.
- An awareness of personal strengths.
- The factors that will help you achieve your goals.
- The barriers that prevent you from achieving your goals.
- Responsibility for your own success or failure.
- Real life actions defined and separated from wishful thinking.
- Encouragement to set priorities and limit distractions.
- The personal victory of goals accomplished and the motivation to succeed in future goals.

APPENDIX 18: PLEASANT AND UNPLEASANT FEELINGS

On this sheet is a list of pleasant and unpleasant feelings. Go through the list (add to it if you want) and tick the ones you have experienced and consider what you were doing at the time. If it was a **pleasant feeling you may choose to do it again.**

Pleasant Feelings

OPEN	HAPPY	ALIVE	GOOD
understanding	great	playful	calm
confident	Jubilant	courageous	peaceful
reliable	joyous	energetic	at ease
easy	lucky	liberated	comfortable
amazed	fortunate	optimistic	pleased
free	delighted	provocative	encouraged
sympathetic	overjoyed	impulsive	clever
interested	gleeful	free	surprised
satisfied	thankful	frisky	content
receptive	important	animated	quiet
accepting	festive	spirited	certain
kind	ecstatic	thrilled	relaxed
	satisfied	wonderful	serene
	glad		free and easy
	cheerful		bright
	sunny		blessed
	merry		reassured
	elated		

LOVE	INTERESTED	POSITIVE	STRONG
loving	concerned	eager	impulsive
considerate	affected	keen	free
affectionate	fascinated	earnest	sure
sensitive	intrigued	intent	certain
tender	absorbed	anxious	rebellious
devoted	inquisitive	inspired	unique
attracted	engrossed	determined	dynamic
passionate	curious	excited	tenacious
admiration		enthusiastic	hardy
warm		bold	secure
touched		brave	
sympathy		daring	
close		challenged	
loved		optimistic	
comforted		re-enforced	
drawn toward		confident	
		Hopeful	

Unpleasant Feelings

ANGRY	DEPRESSED	CONFUSED	HELPLESS
irritated	lousy	upset	incapable
enraged	disappointed	doubtful	alone
hostile	discouraged	uncertain	paralyzed
insulting	ashamed	indecisive	fatigued
sore	powerless	perplexed	useless
annoyed	diminished	embarrassed	inferior

How to use Feeling Very Good as a way into the Happiness Zone

upset	guilty	hesitant	vulnerable
hateful	dissatisfied	shy	empty
unpleasant	miserable	stupefied	forced
offensive	detestable	disillusioned	hesitant
bitter	repugnant	unbelieving	despair
aggressive	despicable	skeptical	frustrated
resentful	disgusting	distrustful	distressed
inflamed	abominable	misgiving	woeful
provoked	terrible	lost	pathetic
incensed	in despair	unsure	tragic
infuriated	sulky	uneasy	in a stew
cross	bad	pessimistic	dominated
worked up	a sense of loss	tense	
boiling			
fuming			
Indignant			

INDIFFERENT	AFRAID	HURT	SAD
insensitive	fearful	crushed	tearful
dull	terrified	tormented	sorrowful
nonchalant	suspicious	deprived	pained
neutral	anxious	pained	grief
reserved	alarmed	tortured	anguish
weary	panic	dejected	desolate
bored	nervous	rejected	desperate
preoccupied	scared	injured	pessimistic
cold	worried	offended	unhappy

disinterested	frightened	afflicted	lonely
lifeless	timid	aching	grieved
	shaky	victimized	mournful
	restless	heartbroken	dismayed
	doubtful	agonized	
	threatened	appalled	
	cowardly	humiliated	
	quaking	wronged	
	menaced	alienated	
	wary		

APPENDIX 19: OTHER TRAINING AND COACHING PROGRAMS ON OFFER:

- Manage yourself to be effective in the workplace program
- Enjoy your job by overcoming harassment at work program
- Happiness as a tool to increase productivity
- Other Personalized programs

A variety of training methods are used in the delivery of these programs. The tools include different instructional methods and ways to provide a positive learning experience with a focus on interactive learning. The methods used range from informative PowerPoint slides that highlight information rather than create visual clutter, flip chart paper for thought shower sessions, use of the participant's real experiences as **live** case studies and homework.

Neuro-Linguistic Programming (NLP) is the science of excellence, studying how people organize their thinking, feeling, language and behavior to produce the results they do. Using this knowledge, the training program will deliver a multitude of new skills, resources and positive behavioral changes for the participant.

1. Manage yourself to be effective in the workplace program

Do you want a new job or more out of your current one?

At work do you feel:

- Undervalued?
- Underpaid?
- That you don't have control over your working day?
- That your manager constantly changes their mind?
- That your manager is unsupportive, puts you under a lot of pressure and sets unrealistic targets?

If the answer is YES to any of the questions above, take action now to get the lifestyle of your choice. Advise us of a time for an introductory 10 minute call.

- During the conversation we will find out what you want to achieve.
- Post call, we will consider your objectives and prepare a personalized package to achieve your goals with the cost.
- Depending on your location, the training part of the package will be delivered face-to-face in a group or one to one, over the phone or via Skype.
- If you are happy to go ahead, we can start as soon as possible.
- Tick the benefits of attending the program that you want to apply to you:-
  - A pay rise.
  - Training opportunities.
  - The chance to learn new skills.
  - A promotion.
  - To have a say in how your work is organized.
  - Flexible working.

Testimonial:

'I used the skills I learnt on the training course and received additional training and several pay increases from my employer' – Ms. W from London.

http://www.feelingvg.com/manage-yourself-to-be-valuable-in-the-workplace-training

2. Enjoy your job by overcoming harassment at work program

I was in a swimming pool at the local gym and a mother, who had taken her daughter for swimming lessons, was telling me how incensed she was with her manager at work. Her manager had accused her of taking drugs. She felt that she was being picked on and had no one to raise concerns with in the company.

I was in the deli section of a large Supermarket. There were six large counter and only one women covering them all. She told me that she had to cover the six large counters on her own and that she had just received a 10p pay cut. She did not think that there was anyone that she could raise her concerns with in the organization.

I once knew an accountant who felt that his manager was treating him so bad that he invited him down to the basement of the building and told the manager to hit him. His manager declined and my accountant friend was suspended from work and eventually lost his job.

As a former manager and area officer within the Citizens Advice Bureau service, I have advised on many work related problems.

Unfortunately, Unions no longer provide the support that workers are looking for.

Employers are responsible for preventing bullying and harassing behavior.

According to the Equality Act 2010 (UK), harassment is unwanted conduct which is related to one of the following: age, disability, gender reassignment, race, religion or belief, sex and sexual orientation and is therefore unlawful.

Unwanted conduct related to a relevant protected characteristic, which has the purpose or effect of violating an individual's dignity or creating an intimidating, hostile, degrading, humiliating or offensive environment for that individual.

Bullying may be characterized as offensive, intimidating, malicious or insulting behavior, an abuse or misuse of power through means that undermine, humiliate, denigrate or injure the recipient.

Examples of bullying/harassing:

- Being picked on and being set up to fail.
- Victimisation.
- Unfair treatment.

- Overbearing supervision or other misuse of power or position.
- Making threats or comments about job security without foundation.
- Deliberately undermining a competent worker by overloading and constant criticism.
- Preventing individuals progressing by intentionally blocking training opportunities.

Visit the following link for more information.

http://www.feelingvg.com/enjoy-your-job-by-overcoming-harassment-at-work

Next steps:

1. Take action now to resolve a difficult situation at work by advising us of a time for an introductory 10 minute call.
2. During the conversation we will find out what you want to achieve.
3. Post call, we will consider your objectives and prepare a personalized package to achieve your goals with the cost.
4. Depending on your location, the training part of the package will be delivered face-to-face in a group or one to one, over the phone or via Skype.
5. If you are happy to go ahead, we can start as soon as possible.

3. Happiness as a tool to increase productivity

"When employees are happy and feel that the company takes their interest to heart, then the employees will take company interests to heart," says Dr. Nelson, a clinical psychologist, best-selling author and business trial consultant.

In her book, Dr. Nelson cites a study from the Jackson Organization, a survey research consultancy, since acquired by Health stream, Inc., which shows that companies that effectively appreciate employee enjoy a return on equity & assets more than triple that experienced by firms that don't.

When looking at Fortune's '100 Best Companies to Work For' stock prices rose an average of 14 percent per year from 1998-2005, compared to 6 percent for the overall market. Give workers balance in their lives; while balancing work life with home life may present a challenge for most workers, it presents an opportunity for companies trying to keep their employees happy. In fact, companies that offer employees a balance between their work and personal lives are more likely to keep employees happy in their current jobs.

Outcomes:
Employer benefits

- Happy workers.
- Employees feeling that they are valued by the organization.
- Increased productivity.
- A loyal and committed workforce.
- Give workers balance in their lives.

Employee benefits

- Motivation to increase productivity.
- Awareness of personal strengths.
- Lifetime Happiness Action plan.
- Steps to create their ideal lifestyle.

1. Take action now to increase your organization's productivity by advising us of a time for an introductory 10 minute call.
2. During the conversation we will find out what you want to achieve.
3. Post call, we will consider your objectives and prepare a personalized package to achieve your goals included in the cost.
4. Depending on where you are in the world, the training part of the package will be delivered face to face in a group or one to one, it

may be by Skype or over the phone. One to one sessions will be delivered face to face or by Skype or over the phone. Depending on your location, the training part of the package will be delivered face-to-face in a group or one to one, over the phone or via Skype.
5. If you are happy to go ahead, we can start as soon as possible.

Visit the following link for more information.

http://www.feelingvg.com/happy-organisations-increase-productivity

4. **Other programs:**

- Workplace mediation.
- Change management.
- Happiness as a tool to achieve a specific outcome.
- Happiness as a tool gain employment.
- Happiness as a tool to achieve a specific outcome e.g. reduce crime.
- Happiness to support ex-offenders.
- Happiness as a tool to address seasonal affective disorder (SAD) from end of autumn and throughout winter.
- Happiness as a tool to reduce depression.

How to use Feeling Very Good as a way into the Happiness Zone

NOTES PAGE

NOTES PAGE

How to use Feeling Very Good as a way into the Happiness Zone

NOTES PAGE

NOTES PAGE

How to use Feeling Very Good as a way into the Happiness Zone

NOTES PAGE

www.ingramcontent.com/pod-product-compliance
Lightning Source LLC
Chambersburg PA
CBHW042325150426
43192CB00004B/118